LAUNCH BIG

**Build a Launch Team,
Launch Big,
Get New Guests
Every Sunday**

BY BRADY STICKER

For my wife Sara. Thank you for being such a massive supporter for me, and a rock that holds our family together.

For my kids, River and Ivory. If God gives you a dream, don't give up on it. He will make it come to pass, if you remain faithful and put in the work.

Table of Contents

While you're reading this book, if you want to learn more about how ChurchCandy can help your church plant grow your launch team, launch big, and get new guests every sunday post-launch; you can schedule a discovery call at churchcandy.com

WHO IS THIS BOOK FOR?

Church Planters (pre-launch)

Has God called you to plant a church? This book will help you build your launch team, launch big, and get new guests every Sunday after you plant.

This isn't for people that want to start a bible study or house church in their living room and see where it goes.

This book is for church planters that want to plant a church, and launch BIG on day one.

What will we cover?

How to use digital marketing strategies to launch your church BIG on day one.

Jesus said in Luke 14:23 "...Go out into the highways and hedges, and compel them to come in, that my house may be filled"

There's never been a better time to go out to the "highways" to compel people to come to church.

You might be thinking "But isn't social media from the devil?"

While yes, I do believe that social media has been a net-negative on society; we can still use it as a means to build the Kingdom. A *take what the enemy meant for evil and turn it for good* kind of approach.

Church Planters & Pastors (post-launch)

While the majority of this book is geared towards church planters before the begin meeting on Sundays, there is still a ton of insight for any pastor or church leader of an established church. The third section of the book is all about how to get new visitors every sunday.

I'd recommend still reading the book from beginning to end, so you don't lack context, and to grab any golden nugget that you can apply to your own ministry.

CHAPTER 1

MY CHURCH PLANT STORY

Cole Hermes and Brady Sticker at Vibrant church's first pre-launch interest parties. March 2nd, 2019

My journey in ministry kicks off just like how many of your stories might begin: growing up in the church, my dad was a youth pastor, and I would play drums most Sundays out of the month from the time I was 13.

In the Summer of 2014, I attended Youth for the Nations (YFN), a Christian Summer camp in Dallas, Texas. It was hosted—and still is today—by Christ for the Nations Institute (CFNI), a Bible college started by Gordon and Freda Lindsay back in the 70s. It was at that camp that I felt the Lord was calling me to full-time ministry. More specifically, He put youth ministry on my heart.

I loved going to youth group as a teenager. I revered my youth pastors greatly, and I really looked up to them. I'd think to myself, *Man, that must be the coolest job in the world.* So, then to have the idea that God might be wanting me to have that job sounded like a dream come true, but it wasn't quite my time yet.

During my first semester at CFNI, my dad reached out and asked me to help him with a business he'd been working on. It was a digital marketing agency for chiropractors called ChiroCandy. He said he'd pay me $50 for every landing page I built for one of his clients. And it took me more or less one hour to build out one of these landing pages. For context, 18 year-old Brady was making $7.25/hour plus tips at a local coffee shop when offered this job. So $50 for about an hours work made me feel like a millionaire.

Granted, it's not like I was setting up forty or fifty landing pages a week, but it was enough to get my attention. Even if it was only three to five landing pages a week, that was enough to pay the bills without having to sling too much coffee.

My dad had actually started ChiroCandy a couple years prior to this, while I was in high school. He wanted me to help him sooner, but my girlfriend at the time—now my wife— worked for her parents' family business and she despised it. I saw how her working for her parents strained their relationship, and I didn't want that to happen with me and my parents. To be fair, their family business was a restaurant, not a digital marketing agency for chiropractors, so apples and oranges, obviously. But still, it took a few months of convincing from my dad to get me on board.

College was a different story, though, and a boy has gotta eat. Proverbs says all hard work leads to a profit and mere talk leads to poverty. I wasn't profiting much at a coffee shop, so I took the job at my dad's company, ChiroCandy.

It started with making landing pages, which led to building out ad campaigns on Facebook, which led to taking sales calls and leading teams. Before I knew it,

I was able to quit my job at the coffee shop to work full time with my dad (at least, as full time as I could while enrolled in school), and I was making decent money, too. It wasn't a crazy salary, but definitely more than what most of my bible college student friends were making.

This got me thinking: Since I was making good money working for my dad, I wouldn't need to work full time at church to get by, or even take a paycheck from one. I could set my own hours at ChiroCandy and then be a volunteer youth pastor part time at a church. I loved the idea of not needing to be dependent on a ministry paycheck to provide for my family, as I know how little and inconsistent those can be for some.

Now, let's skip ahead a few semesters.

Like many Bible school students, I got married young. And remember, this was to the girl who worked at her parents' restaurant. We were living on campus in a humble apartment in Family Housing while I was finishing my studies.

One day I was sitting in my Morals & Ethics class at CFNI when my teacher, Kiplin Batchelor, a lively Jamaican man, decided to stray from the lesson plan, because he felt that God wanted us to spend some time in prayer. Keep in mind this was in Morals & Ethics, which wasn't one of the more spiritual classes at the school. Nonetheless, Kiplin said, "I want you all to seek the Lord and ask Him what He wants you to do after your time at CFNI."

Upon hearing this, I thought, *Easy peasy. I already know what's next for me. I'm gonna work for ChiroCandy and volunteer as a youth pastor at a church.* Simple enough.

But it was in that classroom during that time of prayer when I felt Holy Spirit really impress on my heart that I was called to do more than just be a youth pastor (not that there's anything wrong with being a youth pastor). God was calling me to take everything I'd learned at ChiroCandy and CFNI and use it to build His kingdom by helping local churches grow their attendance the same way we were helping chiropractors grow their businesses.

Immediately after class, I went back to my apartment to tell my wife. And God bless her, she was more supportive than I ever could have hoped, and still is to this day! That was all back in 2018. For the entrepreneurs reading this, I didn't make a single dollar helping churches with their marketing until 2021. Like most God-given dreams, it took some time and a lot of hard work for it to come to pass.

After I graduated from CFNI, my goal was to find a church and serve in its youth ministry, while also helping that church with their marketing. And that would then end up being my very first client.

We interviewed at many churches, and most of them offered me a job as their youth pastor. And if it wasn't for my wife using her God-given wisdom and discernment, I would have said yes to every single one of them. I was fresh out of Bible school, excited to use all the tools I picked up, and the title just sounded really good to me. But after the interviews, when I would tell my wife I wanted to join that church, she would turn to me and ask, "Do you really want to work at this church?" It was always a helpful and sobering question.

My response was typically something like, "Yeah, why not?" Now, I'm not going to dog on any of these churches, but let's just say that my wife has saved me from making many impulsive mistakes with my career. None of those churches were a good fit, and she knew it. So, we continued the search for the right church.

After some months had passed, I came across a Facebook post from someone who had been a spiritual leader in mine and my wife's lives for several years,

Michael Scobey. He was my wife, Sara's, youth pastor when she was in high school, and later did our premarital coaching and officiated our wedding. I'll paraphrase his Facebook post here...

"Hey, we're starting a church outside of Houston, TX in the Spring/Woodlands area. If you want to help, there are two ways to do so: you can join us and move to this new city to launch this church, or you can pray about financially investing in this new ministry."

We called Michael that day to ask more questions. If I'm honest, I was hesitant to move back to the Houston area. I loved Dallas. We'd just started to grow roots there. We were at a wonderful church, we had good friends, Dallas had a lot to offer, and going back to Houston felt like moving backwards in life. After all, an hour and a half drive from The Woodlands to Lumberton, TX where my wife and I were from, was a much closer distance to our family than a five hour drive from Dallas to Lumberton. We were the type of newlyweds who valued our space and independence so we could build our own lives outside the shadows of our parents.

Well, we prayed about it, and God told us to move to The Woodlands to help plant Vibrant Church with Michael Scobey in late 2018. We were the first family other than the pastors themselves to do so. It was our big leap-of-faith moment, if you will.

In the following months, we focused on building our launch team. We hosted "Start-Up" parties and invited other families to join the church plant. This gave me the chance to set up some Facebook and Instagram ads to promote the events. We spent a few hundred dollars on Facebook's native "Event" ads, where people could select if they were interested or planning to attend. Unfortunately, the campaigns didn't work out as hoped. We never got more than one or two people to show up from these ads. Thankfully, we were able to personally invite many locals and make connections with them, but I was still discouraged. I felt like God had given me a vision to help churches with their marketing, but I couldn't even help my own church.

Looking back, I wish I could have used the ad campaigns and follow-up systems we now use with church planters. I believe our launch numbers could have been much higher. But I needed to learn from those mistakes so that others don't have to.

Here's where I went wrong: I used Facebook event ad campaigns where the call to action was simply clicking "Interested" or "Going" on the event without gathering any additional information.

Fast forward to September 2019: Launch Sunday. Over 240 people showed up on day one, and we saw 39 salvations. Praise God. Two weeks later, my wife and I launched the church's youth ministry.

I was finally living the dream, serving as a student pastor without depending on a paycheck from the church. But I knew God was calling me to more.

Just months after our church launched, the world shut down due to the COVID-19 pandemic. Despite the pandemic, I had already made a lot of marketing mistakes. Transitioning from chiropractic marketing to church marketing was both very different and surprisingly similar.

It wasn't until after the 2020 pandemic that we shifted to what's known as Lead Generation campaigns. Now, we had people fill out a form with their name, phone number, and email address, with the call to action being 'Plan Your Visit.' This approach allowed for a much deeper connection.

In June 2020, when we began meeting in person again, Pastor Michael said to me, "Brady, I bet there are lots of people in our city who miss going to church in person." After months of strict government mandates on public gatherings, Texas was one of the first states to open back up. Most people were used to watching church online, but we ran the Plan Your Visit ads, and people responded well, coming back in person.

We used the verbiage, "Plan your visit to Vibrant Church, and you'll receive a free gift and the full VIP experience when you come." Once they filled out the form, we sent automated text messages that were carefully personalized. When they responded, Pastor Michael could text back and forth with them, creating a personal connection even before their first visit.

How many churches offer the chance to text with the pastor before your first visit? It made a huge difference. When new guests arrived, we gave them gift bags with our logo and a tumbler inside that cost about a dollar to make. Even if they eventually threw it away, it worked! We started getting more and more people through the doors.

In June 2020, when we began meeting in person again, Pastor Michael said to me, "Brady, I bet there are lots of people in our city who miss going to church in person." After months of strict government mandates on public gatherings, Texas was one of the first states to open back up. Most people were used to watching church online, but we ran the Plan Your Visit ads, and people responded well, coming back in person.

By September 2020, we had surpassed our pre-COVID attendance numbers. That's when I start getting calls from other church planters who all called to say the same thing:

"Hey, your pastor told me what you are doing at Vibrant and I would love to learn more about it."

Essentially, that is how ChurchCandy was born. We started working with church planters who hadn't even started yet, so we were able to guide them through setting up the right ads with the right formats, all to save them from making any of those initial mistakes that we had made in our infancy months.

And, what do you know, people showed up to their events! And then even more showed up to their Grand Openings/Launch Sundays! I remember the first Grand Opening ad campaign I did for another church planter. They had a launch team of about 50 people, but 350 guests showed up on Day One. The church didn't do a mailer. The only marketing the church did was the Facebook and Instagram ads I set up for them.

Now we have dozens and dozens of testimonies of how God has used social media advertising to bring people to His Church. I just spoke to a church planter last week who recently started having weekly services and he said, "Brady, we baptized 11 people last Sunday, and every single one of them came from the Instagram ads you guys set up for us."

That meant everything to me. That's exactly why I do what I do now, and truly why I believe God has called me into this. Now I lead our social media team at Vibrant—we were able to raise two amazing leaders to take our place in the youth ministry— our church has two campuses, one in The Woodlands and the other in Montgomery, which is an incredible story in itself. And Dad, if you're reading this, I'm sorry but I will never be as passionate about chiropractors as I am about the Church (though, I have a suspicion that you'd be ok with that). There is nothing more fulfilling than helping open the doors for people to come to Christ.

And that's my story—that's how everything led to the launch of ChurchCandy. That's how we planted our church that we still attend. That's how God used me to take social media marketing and further his kingdom with it.

But enough about me. Now it's time to help *you*!

CHAPTER 2

UNDERSTANDING THE 'LAUNCH BIG' CHURCH PLANTING METHOD

Alright, let's get the burning question out of the way: *How do I successfully launch a church with a huge turn-out on day one?* After all, that's the whole implication of this book from the start, right?

In order to answer that, though, we should first prime our mindset with the Launch Big Method, which was discussed above. We'll be using the Launch Big Method as a lens throughout this book to both frame the context of all my strategies and capture the key points I want you to walk away with, so leave your preconceived notions at the door and start thinking like a sponge, because I have a lot for you to soak up.

If you're familiar with the Association of Related Churches (ARC) or the Church Multiplication Network (CMN), you already know exactly what I'm talking about. For those who are unfamiliar with these networks, you should know that between the two of them—over the course of the past 20+ years—they have served as launching pads for thousands of church plants worldwide by equipping leaders and their teams with training, tools, and invaluable relationships with people who have answered the same call. I highly recommend doing your own research of these organizations; their resources are invaluable.

But now, back to answering our burning question! The Launch Big Method focuses on building a team of anywhere from 45 to 85 people who have joined with you in the vision of your church. Those people will then help you utilize your launch funds to make a huge marketing push, with the primary goal of filling as many seats in the room as possible for Grand Opening Sunday, whether that room is a high school cafeteria, a movie theater, or a permanent space you've leased for the foreseeable future.

On Grand Opening Sunday, you host the best church service you've ever attended. That means a prepared worship team, a team with open arms, and solid preaching. Do these things with excellence, and every person who walks into your service is sure to be welcomed by the love of Jesus and the power of the Holy Spirit, and they will remember everything about that experience, including how your church made them feel.

If you can do that, you can launch a successful church. Simple, right? Well, perhaps it is simple, but it is not easy.

Here's why I like the Launch Big Method: to put it simply, it works. By all means, if you want to start with a few families in your living room, I will not discourage you from it. However, gaining momentum will be a much bigger challenge in that situation than it has to be.

Now, let's talk practically. What are the precursor steps to take in order to launch a church from scratch in 18 months using the Launch Big Method?

Step 1: Peace & Confirmation

It is crucial to have spiritual peace in order to plant a church. If God has not called you to this, then your church plant will ultimately fail. It might succeed for a period of time, but if you are not in the will of God with your ministry, any success you experience will be temporary and therefore incapable of producing lasting fruit of a divinely ordained ministry.

Step 2: Location

In what city has God called you to plant this church? In my experience, the most successful church plants launch in up-and-coming suburbs of larger cities.

Brady, are you saying that I can't pitch my tent in the middle of nowhere and have a successful church plant?

Of course not.

Brady, does that mean I have to plant my church outside a downtown square in order to succeed?

That's not what I'm saying, either. I'm saying that once you have divine peace and confirmation about planting your church, your next priority should be *where* you're going to plant it. And unless God has specifically highlighted a city for your church, it is your responsibility to exercise your wisdom, discernment, and due diligence when choosing a location. And there's no better way to find wisdom than to seek it.

Step 3: Seek Wisdom

I always recommend, with everything, even outside of planting a church, to seek wisdom from someone who has already done what you're trying to do.

My son is two years old now, but he wasn't always. And when he was younger, swimming was not in his immediate skill set. He couldn't keep his head above the water if his life depended on it. Very early on, my wife and I decided that it was time for him to learn. Did we both know how to swim? Yes. But did we have any experience in teaching someone how to swim? No. So we looked for someone who did.

As it turned out, there was a lady at our church who taught swimming lessons, so we signed him up. After just a few weeks of bi-weekly lessons, he was swimming better than a lot of adults I know.

Sure, my wife and I could have figured out how to get my son to eventually touch and push in the water, but we valued our son enough to seek wisdom in order to have the greatest success possible.

If you value the church that God has called you to plant, wouldn't it be prudent to look for someone who can bring wisdom and experience to the table?

This brings me back to ARC and CMN, church plant-ing networks who specialize in helping people like you fulfill the special calling God has placed on your life. They have incredible coaching and training that will help you implement the Launch Big Method very, very well. In fact, the majority of the church planters we work with at ChurchCandy have gone through one, if not both, of these organizations' curriculum .

Now that you've found peace and confirmation, chosen a location, and sought wisdom, it's time to build your team.

Step 4: Board of Overseers

Alright, let's dive into assembling your overseer board. Now, this step is closely linked to the previous step, but it's more than just tossing a couple of ques-tions about church planting.

Asking a trusted pastor to be the head of your over-seer board is vital. Because when the time comes to form your launch team, you can proudly announce that you've got a crew of overseers who are pas-tors with thriving ministries all across the map. As a church planter, your role is to tap into your own net-work of pastors who have been there and done that with their own churches.

Picture pastors who've seen more gray on their heads than you've seen on yours, or if you're follicly challenged like my dad, more gray in their beards. You're not exactly asking them to mentor you, but more so to be willing to join in on quarterly meetings. It's like a spiritual support system, having folks who keep you on track.

Now, here's the cool part. Along this journey, you'll most likely cross paths with pastors who've launched churches before you. These seasoned pros can fill you in on stuff you might not even have considered when kicking off a church project. Stuff like: what in the world are your bylaws? Will we associate with a denomination? And let's not forget to find out what it takes to get that nonprofit entity status, the 501c3. Most church planters don't even think about these details until they're staring them in the face.

But here's the kicker: all this wisdom from those who've been through the church planting game before, they've got your back. They can help you correct course when you need it most.

Now that you've laid all the foundation work down, what's next?

Step 5: The Building Phase

I'm not talking about brick and mortar, I'm talking about *people* and *finances*.

- **Building Your Funds**

You know what that means—fundraising! One of the things I love about ARC is they will match you dollar for dollar on your fundraising. If you get approved to plant a church with them, they will match up to $100,000 in funds raised for your launch. You raise twice as much with the same effort. Who doesn't love a double portion? It was good enough for Elisha, it should be good enough for you!

Of course, there are always stipulations, but their only requirement is that you help invest in another church plant, which keeps their initiative running. That's how they continue planting churches year after year!

So, fundraising is a vital part of the building process, but I'm not here to talk all about fundraising. That's another book for another time. The second part of the building phase is...

- **Building Your Team**

If you didn't already know, you cannot launch a church by yourself. End of story. Which means that it is time to start recruiting. You need to double down on vision casting, and get used to saying, "Hey, we're starting a church! Here's our vision, here are our values, wanna help us out?"

This is what it's going to be like: "Would you and your family be willing to attend weekly launch meetings on Sundays instead of attending your church's services for several months so that you can help us start this brand new church? It's going to be life-giving, and a huge blessing to this community, but we can't do it alone." You're basically going to be having conversations like those every single day until you launch the church.

To my knowledge, ARC recommends that you have a team of at least 45 people (specifically 45 adults). If those adults come with children and teenagers, all the better!

Now that you're starting to build a team, that's where this book comes in. One of the key pillars for how we've been able to help hundreds of church planters and pastors build a launch team through social media and digital marketing.

There are two ways to share the vision of your church: One, you have a sit-down, one-on-one meeting with an individual or a couple where you pitch the vision of your church (obviously, you will do many of these). Two, you get a large gathering of interested people into a room and you pitch the vision to all of them at the same time. We call these meetings 'interest parties.'

When my church was in this phase, we hosted an interest party at a coffee shop after hours and bought everyone coffee and pastries. We also hosted a party at a school we were planning to use as our temporary location (but God gave us a permanent space before launch day, and I pray the same thing for you). My favorite Interest Party was at a trampoline park. We rented out a party room where we talked to the adults while their kids jumped and, in the end, we all ended up on the trampolines having fun.

These parties are where you can hand out connect cards, schedule one-on-one meetings, and maybe even sign people up at first sight. And again, if you're connected with a church planting network like ARC, they will help you with these events!

OK, Brady, this is all great... but where the heck are we going to host our services once we launch??

Hang tight! I'm getting there. But before we talk about *where*, let's talk about the *when*.

Step 6: When

When is the best time to plant a church? Personally, my favorite time of year is early September, maybe late August.

Why? It's a season of newness. Besides, when the new school year starts, if a family moves to a new area, they're most likely to do it over the summer, and if they're believers, finding a new home church would be high on their priority list.

My second favorite time of year would be at the beginning, late January or early February. New year launches aren't my favorite, because many church planters lose momentum with their team over the holidays as people get busy with travel and festivities.

But, with that information out of the way, now we can talk about where.

Step 7: Where

Your options are endless here. Your first venue doesn't have to be your permanent venue. The most common places for this type of church plant are school auditoriums, movie theaters, or community event spaces. I've even seen church planters meet in a night club before. Load in Sunday morningn, have service, load out that afternoon. Church by day, disco-tech by night. Any space is a potential venue—Don't box yourself in by traditionality.

Speaking of boxes, if you're planting from scratch, odds are you're going to be loading and unloading a lot of AVL (Audio Visual Lighting) equipment every Sunday, which creates a need for...

Step 8: Storage

Everything from AVL equipment to kids ministry gear will probably spend Monday through Saturday in a storage unit. Then, come Sunday morning, your team will load everything up, haul it to the venue, set it up, and then do everything again in reverse order after service.

This part is a hard sell when you're recruiting. Nobody wants to wake up at 5am on a Sunday, knowing full well they won't be finished working until the better part of 8 hours later, *especially* if your team has young children. It's difficult, but certainly not impossible.

The Church of the Highlands did this successfully for years, and now they're one of the largest churches in America, second only to Life Church, led by Craig Groeschel.

When my church was preparing for our launch, we had our sights set on a middle school for our venue. The school board and administration had signed off, the deposit was paid, and everything was looking settled. But one day, we were selling our vision to a business owner, and when we got to the part where we would be waking up early and staying late every Sunday just to set up and tear down, he looked at us and basically said, "That's nice, but I'm not doing all that on a Sunday. Instead, let me help you invest in a permanent location so you can launch in your own place on Day One."

This, of course, was the most ideal situation. After we ran the numbers, it turned out that the monthly expense of a permanent location was only $200 more than what the school was charging us (also factoring the cost of the storage unit, extra equipment, etc.). All that to say, I encourage you to run the numbers! Don't settle for a temporary venue until you've exhausted all other options.

We were fortunate enough to launch our church in a business complex with a warehouse area in the back that was used for product packaging. We converted that back space into our Worship Center, and the rest was an open lobby with a coffee area, a merch pop-up, and some extra rooms for dream team meetings, kids ministry, etc. You should aim for something similar, that way it's a much easier sell when you're recruiting your launch team. But regardless of what your plan looks like, if you know that God has called you to plant your church, you know that He's going to make it happen.

Here are some things to remember about these volunteers you're recruiting: you are asking them to sacrifice the consistent community from their home church for several months, these people are going to be lobby greeters, kids ministry leaders, worship band members, and everything in between. This is your Launch Team, and for those who stay after the launch and become members, they graduate to your Dream Team.

If you're going to expect this much from your launch team, it is your responsibility to cultivate a new community for them while they are serving within your vision. However, I do not, and I repeat, I do not recommend having weekly services leading up to the launch. As soon as you start holding services, your church is essentially planted. The whole point of following the Launch Big Method is to... well, LAUNCH BIG!

Even if you preface your pre-launch services by telling your team that they are just watered down versions of what your real Sunday services will be like, they're still going to think, "Cool, so this is what Sunday services are going to look like," when in reality, you are not ready for those services yet. If you were, there'd be no need for a Grand Opening.

Does this mean you shouldn't hold acoustic worship nights or designated devotional meetings a couple times a month with your Launch Team before the big day? No! You can absolutely do that. In fact, we did that! They weren't weekly, and we didn't put it on our website, but we kept it consistent for our little community.

Last August I was talking to a church planter—let's call him Paul—who wanted to work with ChurchCandy, but they were preparing to launch their church in January. At that point in the conversation, I knew that rather than growing Paul's church attendance, we would be helping him build their launch team. That's the clear objective if they're six months out from Launch Day.

Let's be clear: Our role as a Digital Marketing Agency isn't to handle all your marketing from top to bottom through social media marketing. Our goal is to use social media marketing as a tool to grow your team, whether you're building your Launch Team, growing your Dream Team, or reaching newer members of the community who are looking for a home church.

I don't care about clicks, reach, or impressions. Anybody can get those. I care about how many people show up to your interest meetings. So when we ran some ad campaigns for Paul, we had 40 families RSVP for the first one, and I believe 10 showed up, which isn't bad! That's 10 families you got to meet in person, with which you had no previous connections. And though 30 families no-showed the meeting, you still have their contact information. And if they were interested once, who's to say they've lost all interest just because they missed the first meeting?

Reach out and ask to schedule a one-on-one meeting with them, or at the very least invite them to the next event!

When Paul hosted his next interest party, he had a very low show rate. Once we had our follow up meeting about the event, we learned that Paul hadn't followed up with any of the families who didn't show up to the last event. Sure, they received some automated text messages and email reminders, but nothing personal. These families filled out a form because they were interested in potentially dedicating months of their life to fulfill the vision God gave Paul for his church, and he never reached out to them. It's no wonder little to no one showed up to the next event; they probably didn't feel any sort of care or connection.

After those events, things started going downhill for the launch plan. Paul wanted to start hosting small Sunday service events before the launch date, and he wanted ChurchCandy to promote them. We advised against it, but he was persistent. So, we ran ad campaigns for these mini services.

At ChurchCandy, we do not cater to the customer-is-always-right mentality. In fact, we oppose it. But here's why we still ran those ads for Paul's services: they are paying our company to promote their church, so we will ultimately honor their wishes, even if they go against our good judgment as the agency. If someone doesn't want to take the advice they paid for, that's on them. But here's the other reason: God might have a special family on His heart, a family that doesn't want to go to an interest party at a bowling alley, or show up to an over-crowded coffee shop, but would show up to a preview service on a Sunday morning. Yes, it went against our better judgment, but we were optimistic that it wouldn't affect their launch.

Then January came around. We reach out to Paul and his team to touch base about running Grand Opening ads, but they respond with, "Well, we're actually going to push back our Grand Opening." Red flag. Still, we accepted the change of plan and revisited the ads in February.

"Hey, Paul! Have you landed on a new launch date yet?"

"Oh, I think we're going to push it back again."

Well, guess what? Paul never did a Grand Opening service. Since they started their weekly mini services, they gained enough momentum to consistently have about a hundred people in their congregation, and they were content with that, so they let us know and we amicably parted ways.

Ultimately, their church was planted, and I'm happy about that. The discouraging part was the potential that was wasted. Had they followed the plan, their impact could have been much larger. More families, more community, more people telling their circles about the story of the Gospel that they heard at a brand new church down the road.

It can be difficult to watch people invest so much time, money, and effort into ARC or CMN, and then into ChurchCandy, growing their Launch Teams and preparing for their big debut, only to sit down ten feet from the finish line.

I always know that God will work through their ministry, regardless of the size and impact, but I can't help but wonder how much bigger their impact would have been, had they stayed the course, listened to their coaches, and stuck to the plan. Where would they be now?

Alright let's skip ahead a little. Six weeks from Launch Day. That's when you want to start meeting with your Launch Team on a weekly basis.

Step 9: Choose Your Leaders

By now, if you haven't already, you should have a pretty good idea of who is going to be leading each serving department in your church, at least for the Launch Team—someone in charge of greeters, kids ministry, worship, etc. You might even have one person overseeing multiple teams. It is not uncommon for high capacity volunteers to wear multiple hats in the beginning stages of a church plant. However, you must be wary not to overload your team, and especially not to take advantage of them. This comes with connection; really knowing the people you're running with. You can't sustain a church that is already burned out on Launch Day.

Step 10: Weekly Meetings

Essentially, you will be training your team, instilling the core values and vision of the church, and sending your volunteers through your growth track that your attendees will eventually take to become members.

Side note: If you're not familiar with the term 'growth track', go check out Chris Hodges' church coaching program called Grow. It will give you all the resources you need for creating your own growth track. This is basically a discipleship/membership class that helps solidify the people in your congregation as members, and get them plugged into a serving team. But for now, it's the prep course for your Launch Team!

The last thing I'll say about your Launch Team is please, if you're able to, bless them. If not with a pay-check, then maybe gift cards, or at least thank you cards. You cannot overlook the sacrifices of these volunteers. A little appreciation goes a long way.

Step 11: The Big Push

You have your team, you have your plan, you're meeting every week leading up to Grand Opening Sunday. Now it's time for the Big Push.

This is when you start spending big bucks on social media ads. This is when you drop $10K-$20K on a promotional mailer for the big day. This is when everything comes into play all at once. The execution.

Let's Recap!

We started with peace & confirmation about our church plant, then we decided a location, we sought wisdom from experience, we established a board of overseers, we started building our team and our funds, we solidified a date and venue for Launch Day, we selected our team leaders, and we sent our team through the growth track.

And that, my friends, is the 30,000ft view of how to plant a church using the Launch Big Method! Give yourself a pat on the back; we covered a lot of ground in these pages. All of these factors are going to ultimately contribute to a smooth, impactful, successful Grand Opening, which will set you up for more growth and expansion in the long run.

Now that we have the big picture, let's take a closer look at how to execute these steps using our proven strategies.

HOW TO BUILD YOUR LAUNCH TEAM WITH DIGITAL MARKETING

CHAPTER 3

COFFEE WITH THE PASTOR

Growing your team comes down to two approaches: recruiting on a one-to-one basis and recruiting on a one-to-many basis. In this chapter, I'll show you the reasons why you should embrace both strategies.

Let's kick things off with the one-on-one approach – the classic Coffee with the Pastor.

As a church planter, if you've heard God's call to reach your city, being open to personal meetings is essential. Of course, I'm all for protecting your calendar and putting your family first. But, when it comes to launching big and building a solid team, those one-on-one meetings are crucial. And while these meetings can happen anywhere, this book focuses on the digital marketing side of things. So, I'll walk you through the digital marketing campaign that can efficiently gather hundreds of people onto launch teams in no time.

Coffee With The Pastor Campaign

Facebook Ad Example   **META Instant Form**   **Coffee Meeting Calendar**

Here's the rundown of what we call the "Coffee with the Pastor" funnel. The first page of this funnel is a simple landing page featuring your calendar. You can easily use tools like Calendly or Church Funnels' calendar booking feature. Include a picture of yourself, or you and your spouse, along with a headline like "Schedule a Coffee Chat with Pastor Brady." This provides a personal appeal to something that might otherwise feel unapproachable.

For efficiency, it's a good idea to hold all these coffee meetings at the same location. If different locations are a must, offer three options across different parts of the city. This has multiple benefits.

Firstly, it streamlines your schedule. You won't be driving across the city; you can just set up shop at the chosen coffee spot. Secondly, it simplifies automated appointment reminders, like follow up texts and emails, when you're dealing with just one location. You have one location listed in all of those "appointment reminder" messages sent out. Thirdly, you have a unique chance to connect with baristas, coffee shop staff, and other regulars to potentially recruit for your launch team. Learn their story, share about Jesus, and share the vission of your church. Coffee shops often have a younger and more open-minded staff, making it a fantastic opportunity for meaningful conversations even outside those you are intentionally meeting.

I know this first hand because I used to work at a coffee shop. Someone invited me to a church, and I attended because I was invited to a life group. So, my suggestion is to pick one coffee shop for these meetings if possible.

After a visitor lands on the initial page, the funnel's next step is a simple form. They pick a meeting time and provide their name, email, and phone number. You will want to keep it minimal at this stage – you're not aiming for a questionnaire. Just simple ways to connect. If you'd like, you could add a question about spouses or other relevant details.

How you *follow up* determines how they *show up*. If they've scheduled a one-on-one meeting but then receive no text reminders, no personal notifications from you, and see nothing on their digital calendars, your show-up rate is bound to be low, or worse, they might not show up at all.

Ensuring your chosen calendar software sends reminders is vital. But also, never underestimate the power of a phone call. Reach out and briefly get to know them. Even if you're planning to spend an hour with them, a phone call is the least you can do. A simple question like, "What prompted you to schedule this chat?" can go a long way in making a connection that is both meaningful and lasting.

It's crucial to get on the phone to humanize the interaction. Show them there's a person behind the messages, someone who genuinely cares. Because if they're only receiving automated reminders, it's easier for them to skip the meeting with what comes across as simply an automation. However, if they sense a personal touch, they're less likely to bail. At worst, they might reschedule, but it keeps the conversation moving in the right direction.

Let's be real here. While it was not my idea, we've invested considerable resources into running our Coffee with the Pastor ad campaign on Facebook and Instagram. This was a concept suggested by one of our ChurchCandy team members. And again, I was skeptical it would produce results. Ads that say, "Hey, I'm new to the area! Do you want to grab coffee and hear about my new church?" felt ingenuine and maybe even a little gimmicky.

Bottom line – I didn't believe this type of approach would actually work. However, one of our core principles at ChurchCandy is putting mission over method. So, if our mission is to aid church planters in growing their launch teams, we're willing to give anything a shot to make it happen. Regardless of whether it was my idea or a team member's.

That's our commitment – to explore every avenue. Don't get me wrong, we have tried-and-true methods that we always start with. But if those methods aren't delivering the desired outcomes, we pivot and explore alternative strategies that also happen to align with the same mission. That's how we stumbled upon this strategy in the first place. That said, I can confidently state that we were among the initial pioneers in renting ads for church planters with the specific call to action of meeting the pastor for coffee.

To my knowledge, we are the first company to ever approach church plant marketing in this way. I acknowledge that there might be others doing it now, but we're among the early adopters of the method.

As a side note, there are church planters who successfully executed the Coffee with a Pastor concept without investing in any ads at all. Here's their approach: They maintained a strong presence on Facebook and Instagram, leveraging local hashtags, engaging in community Facebook groups, and producing content tailored to the local community. They would also occasionally boost posts or promote interest-driven events. Whenever someone interacted with their posts—liked, commented, showed interest in an event—the pastor would extend a friend request on their personal profile. Once accepted, they would send a private message saying, "Hey, I noticed you liked our recent post about our church plant... I'd love to meet over coffee, learn more about you, and share more about our church plant."

This approach demands a significant investment of your time and effort, but it can produce remarkable results. However, what we've seen be even more effective is employing a Lead Form ad on Facebook. In this strategy, we create multiple ad variations, but the central call to action remains consistent: "Grab coffee with the pastor."

These ads could feature an image of the pastor and their spouse, a brief video invitation for coffee, or an inspiring video relating to the church plant where the pastor extends the coffee invitation at the end. The ad text may differ, though, one church planter to another. Crucially, with this approach, we're not sending traffic directly to a landing page with a calendar. Instead, we're leveraging Facebook's lead ad form category. This means we direct traffic to a form hosted on Facebook or Instagram, where we gather essential information such as name, email, and phone number. After they hit submit, they're directed to a page that prompts them to proceed to your website for step two, which involves scheduling coffee. We prefer this two-step process because we've seen that displaying the calendar right away can lead to limited availability, whereas our approach streamlines the engagement.

People might look at the calendar immediately and think, "Oh, there's no suitable time for me. I'll get back to this later." And then, life happens, and they forget about it. Not because they don't care or because they aren't a good fit, but because life's demands take over. The kids have soccer practice, meals need cooking, and daily responsibilities occupy their time. If you begin by asking for their name, email, and phone number, however, using the lead ad approach, you'll gather a significant number of leads. The beauty of Facebook and Instagram lead ads lies in their ability to keep users within the platform. If you've watched *The Social Dilemma* documentary on Netflix, you'll understand the importance of retaining users on these social media platforms.

If your ad redirects them from the app to your website, don't misunderstand me, it's feasible, but it might require a slightly higher investment. However, if you run ads on a platform that retains users on the app while collecting their contact details, they have the option to step out of the app momentarily to schedule a coffee meeting. This approach earns you favor with the platform, and your cost per lead, meaning the cost per form submission, becomes significantly more affordable than if they were directed to your website's landing page with a form.

This strategy is appealing because even if they don't schedule a coffee meeting right away, you still acquire their name, email, and phone number. They didn't accidentally fill out that information after clicking on the ad. This opens the door for follow-up messages, such as:

"Hey, this is Pastor John! I noticed your interest in grabbing coffee. How long have you been in the Sacramento area?"

This initiates a conversation. While the ultimate goal is the coffee meeting, you don't have to be overly insistent in your initial message. Empathize with them, listen actively, and build rapport. Through text messages or phone calls, you'll foster a more positive response, and they will be more likely to say yes when you eventually invite them for coffee or to an interest party.

Even in the worst-case scenario, if they don't attend a coffee meeting, they become part of your email list. When it's time to promote your grand opening launch Sunday, you can invite them to join. Although this isn't a guide on conducting one-on-one meetings or interest parties, here's my general advice: Focus on creating a balanced conversation during these coffee meetings. Ask questions and learn about them. Understand their journey and what brought them to this point. Have they attended church before? How was their experience? Learn why they reached out and sought a connection with your church.

This is when you can transition into sharing your church's mission and vision, tying it back to their story. Avoid the mistake of solely talking about yourself, your church, or your background. Your goal should be to genuinely understand the person across the table. Let the Holy Spirit guide your conversation towards subjects that resonate with them. For instance, if they've had experiences with larger churches, emphasize your sense of community and accessibility.

Towards the meeting's end, ask if they'd consider being part of the launch team. If they're hesitant, encourage them to pray about it. Even after the meeting, if they continue to hesitate, try inviting them to your grand opening service.

Returning to the lead generation approach for booking coffee with the pastor, once people fill out the form on Facebook, including their name, email, and phone number, we recommend setting up an automation. If they don't schedule within 10 minutes, an automated text message is sent from the pastor. Although automated, the pastor engages in real-time if they respond. This approach is transparent and ensures genuine interaction.

The initial message might read: "Hey, this is Pastor John from Vibrant. Is this Brady?" This initiates the conversation. If they respond, you might pre-schedule another message: "I noticed your interest in grabbing coffee. Would you still like to learn more about Vibrant?" From there, manual communication takes over, unless they completely disengage. In that case, a drip follow-up campaign can sustain engagement, touching base once or twice a week over several weeks.

Though there is more to share, this essentially wraps up the Coffee with the Pastor strategy! In the next chapter, we'll dive into all the varying components that lead to a successful Interest Party.

This is a campaign that my team at ChurchCandy has really dialed in. If you want my team and I to set up a full Coffee with the Pastor campaign for your church plant, feel free to reach out. You can schedule a call with the ChurchCandy team at churchcandy.com

CHAPTER 4

INTEREST PARTIES

Now that we've taken a deep dive into the "one-to-one" approach (Coffee with the Pastor), let's pivot to the "one-to-many" strategy for growing your launch team. Interest Parties.

I've heard it called different things (Start-up Parties, Vision Nights, etc.), but the goal is the same; Gather lots of people in a room, give out free food and get childcare, make tons of connections, and then a 10-15 minute vision pitch. No worship band. No 3 point sermon. You'll give people the opportunity after your vision talk to join your launch team.

If you're aiming for a large launch, these interest parties should be front and center. But let's be clear: these aren't your typical worship nights or spontaneous church services. Instead, they're tailor-made events that place community engagement at the core.

Imagine snagging a cozy spot in a park, perhaps a pavilion, and bringing in a couple of food trucks to tempt attendees. Or perhaps you'd prefer booking a lively room at a local restaurant or even renting out a coffee shop after hours to serve up some good conversation alongside steaming cups of coffee. The real essence here is about fostering a sense of community involvement, creating an atmosphere that feels like an open, accessible event. The setup should be designed to encourage mingling and interaction among guests. And as the event draws to a close, take a few minutes to share your own personal journey as well as your church's vision.

Equip your guests with some sort of index cards, inviting them to jot down their contact details—names, emails, and phone numbers—along with a targeted next step for them to take. This could be an invitation to join the launch team, an opportunity to gather more insights about it, or an invitation to RSVP for the Grand Opening. These are some of the essential choices you should put forth.

As you take the stage or address your audience, emphasize the idea that every attendee is there for a reason, not by chance. Stress that their presence is a meaningful contribution. For those who might not be able to commit extensively, consider suggesting their presence at the grand opening Sunday as a way to engage with the church on a more manageable level of commitment. It might be more palatable for them to attend than to join the team, and that works, because they are still getting in the building.

Interest Party Campaign

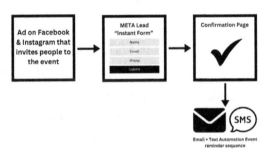

But now, let's shift gears and jump back into the world of Facebook and Instagram ads—an invaluable tool for drawing a substantial crowd to your event. If this is your first rodeo with interest parties, don't be discouraged by the lack of visuals from previous events. You can overcome this hurdle by enlisting a photographer or someone who can capture the event's highlights through professional photos and videos. These visual treasures will become your secret weapon when it comes to crafting compelling promotions for future gatherings.

Now, I get it, you might be tempted to go for a Facebook Event ad... since you're promoting an event. It's a natural thought, but trust me on this one—avoid the Facebook event ad route. Let me share a story from our early days at Vibrant Church. Our very first interest party was promoted through a Facebook event ad. We put in around $500 to give it a boost and the response was incredible. Dozens and dozens of people were marked as going or interested. Sounds promising, right? Well, here's the kicker: **hardly anyone showed up from the ads.**

I made the mistake so you don't have to. The problem with event ads is that they don't let you easily follow up with the people who engage. Unless you're willing to manually add each person as a friend and then initiate DM conversations on Facebook, it's a bit of a hurdle. Frankly, not the most efficient way to handle these ads.

Now, if you still decide to venture down the event ad path, brace yourself for some friend-request-sending exercise. You'll need to go in, add each and every person, wait for them to accept your friend request, and then strike up a conversation in the DMs. Ask them why they RSVP'd, what sparked their interest, and how long they've been in the local area. It's a personal touch, but a time-consuming one.

Quick tip: Make sure they accept your friend request before you dive into the DMs, or else your message might just end up in the abyss of DM requests.

When it comes to promoting events on Facebook, steer clear of the event ad folly. I've been there, I've made that mistake—let's not repeat history. The smart choice is to opt for a Facebook lead form ad. You'll recognize these from our discussion in the previous chapter about the Coffee with the Pastor ad campaign. Instead of whisking users away to a website, these ads direct them to a form right there on Facebook or Instagram. This form is where they can easily enter their name, email, and phone number to RSVP.

And here's the savvy part—Facebook and Instagram thrive on keeping users glued to their platforms. When you drive traffic to an external website, you're kind of taking their users away from them. But with lead form ads, users stay put on their beloved platforms. Not only does this gain you some favor with the algorithms, but it often pre-fills some of the info like name, email, and phone number, which stream-lines the process for those interested in joining.

A word of caution, however: higher volume does often come hand in hand with lower quality. With the convenience of pre-populated forms, some people might inadvertently click submit without realizing they've signed up with their details. And suddenly, they're getting texts and they're puzzled about how you got their info. It's a bit of a double-edged sword in that sense. So, while the quantity might rise, remember that maintaining quality is equally crucial.

Alright, let's tackle this head-on to avoid any unintentional sign-ups. To keep things in check, we incorporate one to two manual-entry questions. It's a simple way to ensure that accidental sign-ups are kept at bay. Take, for example, questions like "How did you hear about us?" or "How many people will be joining you?" — these manual entries add a touch of intentionality to the process.

The key here is to strike a balance between convenience and quality. You don't want to make it a hassle, but you do want to ensure that only genuinely interested individuals are RSVPing. By asking them to manually input a response, it creates a subtle filter to maintain the quality of your leads, and this is an important aspect for maintaining quality responses.

Now, let's focus on making this your primary RSVP collection method. Whatever form you have on your website, make sure it's integrated with the same CRM as your Facebook lead form. Streamlining this process prevents the need to juggle two separate registration lists and eases your management burden.

You've got options for this integration. Zapier can swoop in to connect Facebook form submissions with your Planning Center workflows. If you're seeking an all-in-one solution, consider Church Funnels. It not only syncs seamlessly with Planning Center but also offers superior communication capabilities for text messages and email follow-ups.

And now it is time to dig into the ad campaign flow. Imagine someone stumbling upon your ad, inviting them to a "free community event" or a chance to "discover a new church in Sacramento." Keep the language approachable—avoid church-jargon and terms that might alienate those unfamiliar with church speak. Think of it as a third-grade reading level approach—simple, clear, and universally understandable.

The ad should convey that your church is new in town and ready to connect. It's all about inviting folks to an event loaded with free food, activities, and the opportunity to learn more about your church. If you're not sure how to craft this, even AI tools like ChatGPT can help you generate compelling ad copy with your provided details, but be mindful that those examples will always require a human touch, and should never be used simply as is.

And don't forget visuals. Below are some screenshots of ads that have proven to be effective. Once people engage with your Instagram ad, they'll be directed to an RSVP form through Facebook's lead forms. On the Thank You page, express your gratitude and invite them to learn more about your church by providing a link to your landing page.

Promise City Church
Sponsored · 🌐

Hey Salisbury! 😊
You're invited to our Interest Party!

Hey, my name is Derrick ! My wife Roshonda and I are the lead pastors of Promise City Church. A new, life-giving church launching right here in Salisbury, January 2024!

Promise City exists for all people and for all communities to experience the love of God in everything we do, revealing the heart of God to every person we encounter.

We are excited to invite you to our Interest Party on Sunday, August 27th at 4:00PM! We will have food trucks and drinks for you!

Come hang out with us to hear more about Promise City Church and learn about what we are praying for God to do in our area!

We will be meeting at The Garrison Venue, 1138 Providence Church Rd. Salisbury, NC 28146

Tap to RSVP! 🏃

FORM ON FACEBOOK
You're Invited to our Interest Party! 🎉
Learn more

Promise City Church
Sponsored · 🌐

Hey Salisbury! 😊
You're invited to our Interest Party!

Hey, my name is Derrick ! My wife Roshonda and I are the lead pastors of Promise City Church. A new, life-giving church launching right here in Salisbury, January 2024!

Promise City exists for all people and for all communities to experience the love of God in everything we do, revealing the heart of God to every person we encounter.

We are excited to invite you to our Interest Party on Sunday, July 30th at 4:00PM!

Come hang out with us to hear more about Promise City Church and learn about what we are praying for God to do in our area!

We will be meeting at The Garrison Venue, 1138 Providence Church Rd. Salisbury, NC 28146

Tap to RSVP! 🏃

FORM ON FACEBOOK
RSVP For Our Interest Party! 🏃
Learn more

👍❤️ 41   1 comment   14 shares

👍 Like   💬 Comment   ↪ Share

Watch these video ads here:

When crafting your ads for the interest party, there are two distinct types that you need to consider. First, there are video ads where your excitement for the event shines through. These videos are pure enthusiasm—they're all about showcasing the bounce houses, the fun activities, and the irresistible vibe of the gathering. The key is to create an air of anticipation that nobody would want to miss out on. Emphasize the event's nature as a free community gathering, particularly if it's happening in a park or someplace similar. To broaden the appeal, you could even mention partnerships with the city. This approach ensures that your event doesn't come across as too "churchy" and becomes appealing to a wider audience.

Let's take a look at a remarkable example. Imagine a downtown church planning an Easter egg hunt across the street at the park. By teaming up with the city, they transformed it into an event sponsored by the city itself. The headlines read "Free Community Easter Egg Hunt, San Jose," without heavy religious undertones. This not only attracted a large crowd but also enabled them to connect with 500 people, who later converted to about 5% retention rate the following Sunday. It's an illustration of how making your interest party a significant community event can produce amazing results.

Now, the second type of ad involves imagery from your previous events. The focus here is on showcasing the experience. Show kids and families beaming with smiles, the joy of children bouncing on inflatables, and everyone having an absolute blast. These images will paint the picture of what people can expect at your upcoming event.

The optimal timeline for running these ads is about 14 to 10 days ahead of the event, and here's a budgeting tip: allocate 50% of your ad budget for the four days leading up to the event. This way, you maximize impact just before the event while maintaining a consistent presence throughout the promotion period.

Now, the inevitable question that I am sure everyone wants to ask — how much should you invest in these ads? We've got you covered with a helpful resource available at our **churchcandy.com/calculator**. It guides you through calculating your required budget based on your goals. Let's briefly walk through it:

Start by entering the ideal number of people you aim to attract to the event from using the ads. Consider an average of 2.5 people per family. Estimate your show rate, which heavily relies on your follow-up strategy. Manual follow-up usually results in around 50% show rate, while relying solely on automation could give you around 10-20%.

Next, input your estimated cost per RSVP or cost per lead. This could range from 5 to 25, contingent on your location, event type, and the quality of your visuals. It's worth clarifying that high-quality doesn't necessarily mean ultra HD visuals; rather, it's about effectively communicating your event's essence.

For example, Derrik Hawkins, from the example above, had over 250 people show up to their interest party. Their cost per lead was around $3, thanks to exceptional favor. Others, like Noah Herrin from Way Church in Nashville, had seen a cost per lead closer to

$12. When we're setting up these ads, we try to keep the CPL under $20-30 if possible.

Let's address a common pitfall: Never assume that anyone who fills out a form will automatically show up. It's a mistake we've observed among many church planters. Here's the truth—we've assisted countless church planters, whether in the pre-launch phase or several years down the line, and the ones who achieve the best outcomes are those who understand the importance of proactive follow-up. This applies even before individuals start contributing financially to your church.

Here's a golden rule you can't afford to overlook — how you follow up is how they show up. Text, phone call, email, carrier pigeon - you gotta connect with them, and connect FAST after they RSVP. Many people have phone anxiety and are scared to actually call people and talk on the phone. It's essential to get on the phone with each RSVP. If they miss your first call, try again. If they don't pick up the second time, send them a personal video message where you mention their name and share your excitement about their RSVP. This personal touch goes a long way in fostering connection and boosting their possible attendance. Here is what to say in these videos:

"Hey {FIRST NAME}! This is pastor {YOUR NAME] from {CHURCH PLANT NAME}. I saw you just RSVPd to our {EVENT NAME}. We're looking forward to seeing you there. Feel free to reach out if you have any questions or prayer requests."

Additionally, automation is a must for sending out emails and texts as reminders about the event. However, it's crucial to avoid relying solely on automation as your only method of follow-up strategy. Think of it as a safety net, not a total replacement for personal care. While you might not have your church fully established yet, even before your building or Sunday services, remember that pastoral care should already be in action.

At this stage, the goal is to make everyone feel seen, valued, and important. You won't necessarily lead them to a complete turnaround or solve their spiritual or life problems instantly, but that's okay. Jesus demonstrated this approach throughout the Bible. Think of the woman at the well—she wasn't made to feel small or unimportant. Similarly, you can start by making people feel seen, heard, and appreciated. Remember, the woman at the well was initially seen as an outcast, but Jesus prioritized love over judgment. He made her feel significant, even before she arrived at his side. So, your focus should be on making people feel important and loved, well before they even attend the event.

As for a basic automation plan, it depends on how far in advance you start promoting. Generally, consider sending a text and email one week before the event, followed by another set three days before, two days before, one day before, and even a morning-of text and email. This approach creates a safety net of communication, but remember, it's not a crutch.

In summary, while automation helps maintain engagement, it should complement, not replace, personal connections. Just as Jesus prioritized love and empathy, focus on making each individual feel valued and significant—a practice that sets the stage for a fruitful and genuine engagement with your church community.

In a later chapter, we'll dive deeper into optimizing your ad campaigns for the best outcomes, regardless of the type of event you're promoting.

The ChurchCandy team and I have set up 100+ interest party campaigns. If you'd like us to help you with this process, we can do it for you. Just schedule a call with the team at ChurchCandy.com.

CHAPTER 5

DIRECT MESSAGE OUTREACH

We've seen time and time again that the more people you have on your launch team, the bigger your launch will be. And social media is a great opportunity for you to prospect potential leads for launch team members. Not just leads that RSVP for an interest party or fill out a form saying they're interested in grabbing coffee, but anyone that likes, comments, or engages with any of your social media ads or organic posts. These are all potential launch team members, period.

If God has called you to plant a church, you have to understand that it's not going to be easy. The first step of building that launch team is going to take a lot of work. It will take a lot of effort on your end to make genuine connections with people. And you have to essentially become a salesman.

Now, I know that might make some people feel sleazy, but it's true. You're becoming a salesman because you're selling the idea of a church before your church is ever even there.

There is a difference between a good salesman and a bad salesman. A bad salesman is what people refer to as a used car salesman. These are people who take advantage of others, selling things that are too good to be true or things people don't need. However, a good salesman only sells things they know their prospect actually needs and can benefit from.

For example, at ChurchCandy, we coach our sales team not to be salespeople, but to be consultants. To learn about pastors and church planters, where they're at in their journey, and if we can even help them at ChurchCandy. Then, if we can help, it's their job to just explain how ChurchCandy can help their church. We turn away many pastors and church planters because we are just not a good fit. We only take on new clients if we are 100% certain we can help them.

What does this mean for you and your church plant? You have to sell the vision. You have to sell the idea of a church and what it's going to be like Sundays, weekend in and weekend out, six to twelve months before you ever have Sunday services. You have to get people bought in to early morning set ups for a portable church. You have to sell the idea of investing financially into the church. And that's a hard thing to do, but that's why it's important to be a good sales- man and not a used car salesman.

If you truly believe in the vision of your church and what God has called you to, then it's going to be super easy for you to be a good salesman, because you know the value that your ministry will give to the fam- ilies you're trying to sell into joining your launch team.

One of the best church planting strategies I know of is completely free. All it takes is your time. This strat- egy involves creating organic social media posts or running ads. Anytime someone likes or follows your church on Instagram or Facebook, you immediately follow them back and start a conversation in the DMs.

You have to be very tactical about this. If you just set up an automated message that goes out to everyone who follows you, or if you just copy and paste the same message to everyone, you won't see much fruit from this strategy. But if you're super intentional and take the time, anytime someone likes or comments on any of your content, or especially the people that fill out forms either RSVPing for an interest party or wanting to get coffee, you need to treat that as an open invitation to make a connection.

Think of it as running into someone at the grocery store and starting a conversation about your new church plant. It is your job then to make a personal, authentic connection with them with the hopes of scheduling a one-on-one meeting so you can really pitch and sell the vision of your church plant.

For social media, whenever you're connecting with people on there, make sure that if they like any of your content on Facebook, you add them as a friend. Once they accept your friend request, move into the DMs. One of the easiest DMs you can send is simply their first name with an exclamation point. Just call out their first name. Do this from your personal account, not the church's public page. Then, spend 30 seconds scrolling their social media profile to learn about them. Do they have kids? What line of work are they in? Then ask them about it.

"I see you have three kids. I've got two myself. We just moved to the area. How do you like the schools here?" Or, "I see you're an engineer at this company. How do you like that? My brother does the same thing."

Start a conversation. Be intentional about building a relationship. Your goal should be to set up some sort of meeting, whether it's lunch, coffee, or something else. Hopefully, you're already used to doing one-on-one coffee meetings through your Coffee with the Pastor ad campaigns.

On Instagram, ideally, you want them to follow you back so your DMs are more likely to show up in their inbox and not land in spam. Follow the same strategy on Instagram. Ideally, do it from your personal profile, but it's not as crucial as it is on Facebook. Just make it clear you are who you say you are, the pastor, and not talking as the church overall. "Hey John, this is Michael, the pastor from Vibrant," for example.

One thing I love that Josh Whitlow from Purpose City Church in Phoenix, Arizona did when he launched his church is he would prioritize getting as many of these one-on-one coffee meetings as possible. Even if someone RSVP'd for an interest party, if he looked them up on social media and they seemed like a high-quality potential launch team member, he would really work that lead by sending personal texts and phone calls to nurture the relationship and try to meet up with them for coffee or lunch before the interest party happened.

This is going to take a lot of work. It's not going to be easy, and it's going to take a lot of time. But the more connections and authentic relationships you make on social media, the more one-on-one coffee or lunch meetings you'll have where you can pitch your church plant. The more one-on-one meetings you have, the more new potential launch team members you have. It's going to take work, hustle, and grind.

Galatians 6:7 says, "A man reaps what he sows." If you don't put much effort into making personal connections, you're going to have a hard time building your launch team. But if you highly prioritize making personal connections and using social media as a way to form these connections, you're going to see a lot more fruit from this strategy.

CHAPTER 6

DON'T GET A WEBSITE! DO THIS INSTEAD...

Being a business owner, I meet all sorts of entrepreneurs and *want-repreneurs* alike. And if you're planting a church from scratch, chance are, you've got that entrepreneurial bug as well. Maybe even tried your hand at some side hustles in your spare time.

Now, the hiccup I see most people stumble on is this: they get caught up in stuff that doesn't actually push their main goal forward. For example, I run a digital marketing agency for churches. But if I'm starting up "ChurchCandy," and I burn hours on logo design, fussing over website domains, and going nuts perfecting the website – yeah, all those things are good, no doubt, but sinking hours into a logo design won't directly bag me a new client. Hours spent crafting a website won't magically conjure a thriving Church-Candy. For context, we didn't even have a website, logo, or even a company name until after we already had about 20 clients.

When you're just getting your digital footprint off the ground for your church plant, you want to start with what we call an MVP; Minimum Viable Product. Do the least amount of build out as possible that gets the job done. You need a church name, that's a yes. You need a snazzy church logo, that's another yes. But what are some of the things that you DON'T need for your church? But there is no need for a 30-page website or social media accounts on every platform known to mankind.

What you really need in your pocket right now – the big three: Facebook, Instagram, and YouTube. This may change in the future, but at the time of writing this, those are the three that have the most impact for your church. The rest? Not a big deal when you're just kick-starting.

So, where should your focus be? Here's the deal when you're booting up your church plant: go all-in on building your launch team. Don't get tangled up chasing after the flawless website, or sweating over your logo's color palette.

When most people fall into this trap, it's because they're dodging the real deal – actions that rope in folks and lock them into your launch team. Remember, you don't need a full-on website before liftoff. For your digital footprint's minimal, viable vibe, you're aiming for a landing page, not a full-scale website. Landing pages keep it sleek, usually with one main action. While it's possible to sneak in a couple more actions, let's not go overboard – a maximum of three calls to action for a landing page.

So, about this page – it's your one-stop-shop for everything about your church plant. City location? Check. Grand opening date or at least a ballpark season? Got it. Toss in a video where you spell out your vision, mission, core values, and why you're diving into church planting in your city. If you're following ARC's full playbook, you'll probably like the "know God, find freedom, discover a purpose, and make a difference" mantra.

Now, let's dive into calls-to-action. These are the next steps, the nudge that's everywhere, even if you don't notice it. Facebook? The call to action there? Creating an account. Domino's website? Call to action? Order online.

Your church website, post-launch? "Plan your visit." For the pre-launch, team-building stage? Let them learn more about the launch team. That could mean snagging a chat with the pastors, RSVPing for an interest party, or simply staying in the loop with church updates.

Quick note, these calls to action get less personal as you move down the line. One-on-one coffee chats with a pastor – pretty personal. RSVPing for an interest party – less personal, but still a commitment. Staying in the loop – low commitment. So when you're building that landing page, your star player should be that one-on-one coffee chat. It's front and center, in the hero section. Unless you're two weeks away from an interest party – then you can flip the script, focusing on RSVPs.

And remember – high-quality pics mean a top-notch digital footprint. For your landing page, for your church plant, make sure you're bringing your A-game. Whether you're preaching or hosting an event, get a photographer on board. And these days, vertical video is superior on social media – so if your photographer can capture that, it's a double win.

Follow-up is and always will be your secret weapon. Because, remember: **How you follow up is how they**

show up. That's the core of what we do – getting folks to show up. Whether it's coffee chats, interest parties, social gatherings, or Sunday services, nailing the follow-up is key.

When someone fills out a form, don't let it collect virtual dust. Reach out, strike up a conversation. If it's a "learn more" form, that's your cue for a chat about their interest. Ideally, the top dog on your calendar is scheduling those one-on-one coffee meetings. But there should always be allowances for wiggle room here and there.

Trust me, if you're not bi-vocational and this is your gig, one-on-ones are your bread and butter. We'll dive deeper into how to line up those meetings, but for now, just remember that every form is an opportunity.

Here is an overview of establishing your digital presence for a church plant. Save these insights as you prepare for your launch day. Maintain a clear focus, and we will continue to explore additional valuable information in the forthcoming chapters.

CHAPTER 7

ORGANIC SOCIAL MEDIA (PRE-LAUNCH)

One of the most common questions I get at Church-Candy is: What should I be posting on social media? Whether you are a pastor with a long-standing church or someone starting a new church, this question is important. If you already give sermons every Sunday, you have a lot of good content you can use to make interesting posts for social media during the week.

However, if you're in the startup phase, you're likely not in the pulpit every Sunday just yet. This puts you at a disadvantage compared to the established churches. So, what can you do instead?

Here are the key types of content you should be organically posting on your social media platforms:

1. Showcase Your Church as a Community: Treat your social media pages as an extension of your church landing page. When someone stumbles upon your Instagram profile, you want them to get a taste of the vibrant community that thrives at your church. Keep in mind, since you're not holding regular Sunday services at the moment, you won't be able to necessarily showcase some of the more liturgical elements of worship. Instead, focus on highlighting the sense of community fostered during interest parties and other gatherings.

2. Create Uplifting Talking Head Videos: Compensate for the absence of spiritual content that established churches can readily share by crafting encouraging talking head videos of various lengths. In these videos, you can offer spiritual advice, share nuggets of wisdom, or narrate stories to provide encouragement.

These are both great opportunities to hone your storytelling skills. Now, bear in mind, trends in video formats may change over time, but the principles I'm about to outline should remain applicable, regardless of the format or type of content you're creating.

For vertical videos, the initial hook in the first couple of seconds is crucial. You want to say something that compels viewers to pause their scrolling. A common mistake I've noticed some pastors make is to introduce the video topic and then dive straight into a story. For instance, if the video is about cultivating faith during challenging times, they might start with, "Today, we're discussing how to have faith in troubled waters," often delivered in a monotonous or preachy tone.

Here's a more engaging approach: Begin with a hook and then go straight into a captivating personal story. *"Do this next time you're needing faith in a hard time. When I was [X] years old I..."*

This immediately captures your audience's attention and draws them into your story.

The importance of the hook cannot be overstated because its primary function is to halt the endless scrolling of viewers. TikTok, in particular, has ushered in an era of incredibly short attention spans. I've even found myself guilty of this trend. When a video fails to captivate me within the first few seconds, I instinctively continue scrolling, searching for the next source of instant gratification.

This culture of brief attention spans requires a special approach when creating video content. Stories should take center stage with minimal fluff. Always remember that viewers' patience is limited, so it's crucial to avoid monologues that drone on for even the simplest of two and a half minutes. Presently, social media algorithms place considerable weight on video retention. High retention rates send positive signals, while swift viewer departures after just a couple of seconds indicate disinterest, resulting in algorithms devaluing your video.

Now, let's delve into the realm of calls to action (CTA) in these encouraging videos. I firmly believe that every video should feature a CTA. However, most of these CTAs shouldn't be focused on immediate actions, such as, "If you're in the Sacramento area, join our interest party next Tuesday." Instead, the majority of your CTAs should revolve around simpler actions like "give me a follow," "like and save this video," or similar prompts.

Social media algorithms employ discovery algorithms, meaning your content will reach individuals even if they don't follow you. This implies that people from diverse locations, both national and international, will stumble upon your videos. Keep this in mind when crafting your content. While these videos won't single-handedly fill your launch team, they will gradually build a following and establish social proof.

Additionally, when local residents visit your Instagram page, they'll gain insight into your personality and pastoral style.

Now, if you consistently mention that your content is geared towards a local audience, you may risk lower retention or viewer disinterest. Therefore, if you aim to gain followers and amplify your influence, consider producing these uplifting videos without emphasizing their locality.

Local-oriented videos, on the other hand, adopt a more community-centric tone and minimize their spiritual aspect. For instance, a community-focused video could highlight the "Top Three Mexican Restaurants in Sacramento." Share your favorite spots and showcase their delectable dishes, all while subtly mentioning your role as a pastor launching a new church in Sacramento.

Here's an example of how to integrate this:

"Let's talk about my top three favorite Mexican restaurants in Sacramento. First up is [Restaurant Name]. Their grilled al pastor is a must-try. And, as a pastor launching a new church right here in Sacramento, I couldn't resist savoring some al pastor myself."

Feel free to leave out the dad jokes if it's not your vibe. You can include a casual mention at the end: "If you're in the Sacramento area and curious about our new church, check out our other videos for more info."

This approach allows you to strike a balance between subtly promoting your church and delivering engaging content. When you employ local hashtags and tag local businesses, such as shops or restaurants, your videos gain visibility. These businesses may also share your content with their audiences, broadening your reach.

Finally, your social media content should feature images and videos from your interest parties. I recommend organizing at least one worship night, even if it means renting a space in another church to simulate the atmosphere you envision for your launch. Capture visuals of the event's setup and ambiance. This will serve as a placeholder for the spiritual aspect of your content, ensuring your social media presence isn't solely promotional. Strive for an 80-20 ratio with your content: 80% of your content should provide encouragement, value, and messages like "Jesus loves you in Sacramento as in heaven," while the remaining 20% can focus on event promotion.

As you approach the 30-day mark before your launch, it's acceptable to intensify your promotional efforts. However, maintain a 60-40 ratio with your content at that point, with 60% dedicated to encouragement, value, and general content, and 40% dedicated to promoting your grand opening. During the launch week, you can slightly shift the balance to 60% promotion and 40% value content. This ensures a well-rounded social media strategy that effectively engages your audience.

HOW TO LAUNCH BIG WITH DIGITAL MARKETING

Grand Opening Promotion Strategy

CHAPTER 8

LAUNCH ADS VS. MAILERS

It was our church's first "youth lead service". I was the student pastor at the time, so I got to preach, and the band was almost all teenagers. We had students serving all through out the church that day; from greeters to the sound booth.

After the service, a man I had never met before came up to me. I could tell he was a first time visitor, because he was carrying one of our *new-guest bags* (a tell-tell sign). After introducing himself, I asked what I ask every first time visitor; "How did you hear about Vibrant?"

I'll never forget his response.

"Pastor Brady, I knew God was calling me to Vibrant, because everytime I turned around on Instagram, I kept seeing you guys!"

My face was filled with a grin, from ear to ear. I responded, "Amen brother! I believe God wanted you hear for a reason."

It was working. We had started testing instagram and facebook ads that were specifically targeting people that had already watched any of our videos or been to our website. So after META saw someone was interested in our church, we would "follow" them around on social media with these retargeting ads.

A mailer can't do that. That's only possible with social media ads.

Today, church planters and pastors that work with ChurchCandy often tell me that new guests say the same things.

When it comes to promoting your church plant's grand opening, there are a variety of routes you can take. You might consider running a Facebook event ad or go classic with mailing postcards to every home within a five-mile radius of your church. Heck, I've even heard of church planters with a generous budget going all out with tv commercials, billboards, and LED sign trucks. These are often referred to as "weed trucks", as they're a popular advertising medium for marijuana dispensaries. The church planter told me that, *"if it's good enough for weed shops, it's good enough for the lord."*

That church planter had a 4 figure launch (1,000+ people in attendance).

Honestly, there's no one-size-fits-all approach to promoting your grand opening church service. But there are ways that tend to be more effective than others.

The most common method for promoting a church plant's grand opening is through mailers. I talk to church planters and pastors regularly, and it's not unusual for someone to say something like, 'We're not doing mailers because they don't work anymore.' Let me clarify - I'm not anti-mailer at all. I actually believe in their potential. After all, when was the last time you received physical mail that wasn't just a scammy car warranty offer?

People do still notice something tangible in their mailbox.

There are two ways to ace mailers. The popular approach involves beautifully designed postcards that tease the recipient. It might say something like, 'This piece of mail could change your life,' and on the flip side, 'Well, not quite, but it's an invite to our new church.' These postcards pack the event details and an open invitation to join. They work because people tend to think, 'Oh, look, mail!' It's a physical touchpoint that makes an impression.

In fact, even the ARC recommends investing in mailers. They recognize the power of this strategy.

Now, here's an innovative spin on a direct mail campaign that I haven't personally tried but have heard of others finding success with - handwritten letters. Before you skip ahead, hear me out. You won't be penning these letters yourself; and you won't need your team to do it, either. There are companies out there with machines that can mimic human handwriting. These robotic scribes craft letters that can be tucked into envelopes that resemble birthday cards from your grandma. It's personal and different, and I've heard it can work wonders.

If you're intrigued, a quick Google search for 'handwritten letters direct mail campaigns' should lead you to resources on how to get started. If you choose this route for your mailer, make sure to shop around for the best deals and not overpay for the personal touch of a handwritten letter.

Let's be clear; mailers can be effective in getting people to show up. The real challenge isn't whether they work; it's about how well they work in proportion to the money spent. In the business world, we call this 'return on investment' or ROI.

Let's break it down. Imagine you invest $10,000 on a mailer that reaches 3,500 homes within a 5-mile radius of your church. Out of those 3,500, let's say you achieve a 1% conversion rate, which means 35 families show up for your launch. If you assume 2.5 people per family, that's about 90 individuals attending your church.

Math time. You spent $10,000 and got 90 people to visit. That means you shelled out around $285 for each family that walked through your doors. Don't get me wrong; every life changed is priceless, and leading someone to Jesus is beyond measure. However, we're also called to be responsible stewards of our church's finances. There are more cost-effective ways to reach people for your grand opening service beyond using mailers.

As an example, let's look at Austin Scott, who is the pastor of a brand new church in Lexington, South Carolina. So, Austin launched within a town of about 20,000 people, and their story is quite a wild one.

They had set up a mailer just prior to their launch, it cost them around $14,000, and it was supposed to go to every single house (give or take) in Lexington County because they wanted to make sure that absolutely everyone knew that services were starting. All good things, until the week before launch, they got a call from the mailer printer who said there was a disaster on the printing floor, and the mailers were not going to get out at all.

It was around this time that ChurchCandy had started to come alongside them, and with that $14,000 back in their bank account along with the work that we did with them to get things up and rolling prior to this issue, they were able to have over 450 people show up for their launch Sunday, which is amazingly massive for that area!

Austin says that "they put a lot of groundwork and stuff in before... but when it comes to marketing, there's nobody better than ChurchCandy... having that many people show up was awesome, and yeah, you can't do that with just a little postcard. No, it's about relationships".

When you're gearing up to run ads for your church's grand opening, it's all about choosing the right platforms – think Facebook, Instagram, TikTok, and

YouTube. These are the spaces where you can laser-focus on folks based on where they live and what tickles their fancy. None of that waiting around for someone to Google 'church near me' and stumble upon your ad. So, my advice? Save Google ads for later, like when your weekly Sunday services are in full swing.

Now, after dropping big bucks on ads for countless churches and even a few chiropractors, and partnering with over a hundred church planters, here's the scoop: Facebook and Instagram, both under the Meta umbrella, are the true champs. From now on, I'll refer to this powerhouse duo as Meta, which covers both platforms. If it's strictly Facebook or Instagram-related, I'll keep it real and name-drop them separately.

Running ads on Meta is your golden ticket to the best return on investment (ROI) when it comes to filling up your grand opening venue. Ideally, you've already splurged a bit on promoting events like interest parties and cozy coffee meetups with your friendly neighborhood pastor about a month before your launch. But if you haven't, don't sweat it. You can still get by without them. However, if you've been investing heavily on ads, one of my personal favorites is the 'retargeting' strategy. Retargeting is the strategy I tell at the beginning of this chapter.

Here's a simple explanation: Retargeting is just showing ads to people that are already familiar with your church. You can show ads to anyone that has watched your videos, visited your website, or even anyone that clicked on an "Interest Party" ad, but didn't , we send them more invites to your grand opening.

If you haven't started inviting people yet and you're still getting ready, here's what to do: First, make videos for your ads instead of just using pictures. Second, make sure your website or landing page has the Meta tracking pixel. This helps us show ads to people who already know about you. They might be interested, and the Holy Spirit might be guiding them to your new church.

You might chuckle or think people, but there's some truth to it – the Bible talks about sowing seeds, not necessarily reaping the harvest every time. So, when we're tossing money into the social media ad garden, we're really just planting loads of seeds. We can't expect a bumper harvest every single time, but what we can do is trust that the Holy Spirit will do His thing, nudging people, inspiring them, and leading them to your church.

CHAPTER 9

HOW TO USE ADS TO LAUNCH BIG

There are unlimited ways to promote a church's Grand Opening. From mailers, billboards, social media ads, there are endless possibilities. Or, you could do what my friend, Mike Santiago did when they launched Focus Church in Raleigh, North Carolina. Here's his story from our interview on the ChurchCandy podcast:

I hired a kid to dress up as Satan. And he flipped a sign that read the words, "I hate focus church.com" and Ihate-focuschurch.com was a domain name that I owned and it pointed people to a splash page where I had shot a video that just simply said, "Hey, you probably saw Satan on the corner, you know, protesting our church. And the reason Satan is protesting our church is because it's a church that Satan hates because it's a church that you're going to love."

Disclaimer

I'm sharing this because of how funny the concept is. I'm not necessarily recommending that you do this or something like it.

It is your responsibility to be a good steward of what you have. Which means nailing down how much you should invest for mailers, promotions, and personal invite cards, as well as how much you're going to spend on Facebook and Instagram ads.

But let me kick off by sharing a story from Pastor Brian Bullock. He was on the pulse of launching a fresh church, a campus of Union Church led by Pastor Stephen Chandler. It's a cool setup – an independent campus with Pastor Brian preaching every Sunday, situated in a whole different city from the main Union Church campus. What made it even cooler was their sending church's involvement. They rolled in to help them raise the needed funds – covering Brian's paycheck, securing a venue, snagging gear for the kids' ministry, decking out the worship service with AVL equipment, and so much more.

So, when they took off with ARC, a standout feature was ARC's fundraising aid. And here's the juicy part – ARC's all for it, ready to match funds up to $50,000 (before they raised it to $100,000). And so here's the play: Pastor Brian and his crew waved their magic wand and funneled every bit of that ARC cash into their marketing stash. Meanwhile, the sending church took on the role of superhero, raising funds for everything else. They said, "Let's pour this into outreach," and that's exactly what they did. Their moves included buying out an ice cream joint, treating everyone and sparking conversations, all while slipping a card to the cashier – a little invite to Union Church Charlotte's Grand Opening.

You might be thinking, "Okay, fifty grand for launch marketing? That's some serious cash." And you're right! I know some church planters who've launched with only fifty grand in total. But guess what? It all paid off. It was a real-life lesson in sowing and reaping. Now picture this: a whopping 1,700 people showing up to Brian's very first service, their grand opening. The equation's clear – the larger the marketing budget, the larger the launch. You can't just count on having a massive launch team, thinking they'll bring all their buddies and their buddies' buddies.

Now, let's be fair – social media marketing shouldn't replace an invite-culture. But people only know so many people. It's a bit like the 80/20 rule – 20% of your effort gets 80% of the result. They poured their heart and soul into building that launch team. It was a time-consuming journey, pouring into lives, nurturing connections through coffee chats, hosting many interest parties – the whole deal.

But when the rubber met the road, most of the crowd that streamed in didn't march in because they knew a launch team member. It was a different game. They'd seen Pastor Brian's face on social media, spotted those billboards, and even gotten church invites in their mailboxes. It's like a marketing golden nugget – it takes about 7 exposures for someone to make the decision to jump in. And they did not skimp on getting all those different types of marketing goldmines in front of everyone's faces.

That rule of thumb applies to your ministry as well. Don't be disheartened if people don't show up the first time you extend an invite. It's a bit like a sequence of events – you see the church on a billboard, then a Facebook ad pops up, followed by an Instagram video ad, and an invitation in the mail. All these strategies work together holistically, eventually leading to a big launch.

As you're reading this, odds are you're not necessarily aiming for a mind-blowing 1,700-strong crowd at your service. Most of you would be thrilled to see 170, 270, or 370 folks at your grand opening. Our roster of church planters tends to allocate about three to five grand in ads for their big day. On average, the church planters we collaborate with pull in just over 450 attendees on their opening Sunday.

Of course, there's always an exception to the rule, like Pastor Brian. To be clear, I'm not claiming credit for all 1,700 attendees, but I know that it was a blessing to have been able to play a substantial part in that turnout for them.

You know what that means; it's time to whip out the trusty tool I told you all about – the ChurchCandy Calculator (churchcandy.com/calculator). It's your magic wand to figure out the money game: how much cash do you need to allocate based on the number of folks you want to see at your church? Input the direct headcount you're aiming for from your ads. Keep in mind, this number represents individuals, not families. The next query asks you to estimate how many people you expect to arrive with each family.

We usually see an average of about 2.5 individuals per family, but if your demographic swings towards the mature end, that might drop a bit. Conversely, if your church is bustling with young families and their bundles of joy, that number might spike. But for most cases, 2.5 gets the job done when I'm running the calculator with churches.

The third question dives into your show rate, or in simple terms, how many people will actually turn up. And the fourth one? It's all about the cost per lead or cost per submission for your grand opening Plan Your Visit form. This is where you slice and dice – take the cash you invested in ads, and slice it by the number of families that joined the **plan your visit** form party.

Now, when it comes to grand openings, the excitement around its novelty and starting from scratch usually translates to lower costs compared to ongoing promotions of weekly Sunday services. Based on our findings from churches utilizing the ads we dive into in this book, they typically allocate around $10 to $15 per family for planning a visit to their grand opening.

Nevertheless, we've encountered instances where some allocate closer to $1.50 per family for form submissions, while others invest as much as $25 to $35 per lead. The variance in these numbers is largely influenced by ad optimization and regional factors. To achieve optimal results, which we'll discuss in more detail later in this book, we focus on honing our ad strategy to lower these costs.

Upon inputting all the relevant data into the Church-Candy Calculator, you'll receive a recommended ad budget tailored to your provided inputs.

Our Grand Opening strategy closely resembles our approach to Facebook and Instagram ads for coffee with a pastor and interest party campaigns. The primary distinction lies in the sheer volume of variations we create due to the typically higher budget allocated to these campaigns. Furthermore, we employ more retargeting, ensuring that ads are directed at individuals who have previously engaged with us.

To kick start the process, it's advisable to construct a Facebook Meta lead ad rather than simply directing traffic to your website (For more information on lead ads, please refer to the relevant section earlier in this book).

Given the substantial budget, diversification is key. To illustrate, I previously introduced the concept of the Shotgun Strategy in my book, "Plan Your Visit Playbook." The analogy behind this approach is rooted in my Texan background – much like going duck hunting with a shotgun rather than a rifle. The shotgun approach entails casting a wider net by creating numerous ads, each boasting distinct elements such as images, ad text hooks, videos, and headlines. The aim is to maximize the chances of resonating with the intended audience.

This strategy facilitates scalability and optimization. After a few days of running the ads, we can evaluate their performance and deactivate those that aren't yielding favorable results.

In my experience, initiating launch ads with a modest budget about 30 days before the event and progressively increasing the allocation daily tends to help in yielding effective outcomes. I recommend commencing your launch ads with a modest budget, a month in advance. Subsequently, gradually increase the daily allocation as each day passes. As you approach the launch date, around two weeks prior, that's when you should implement your maximum daily ad spending budget.

If you've got a thousand bucks to spare, crunch the numbers. Imagine you're motivating your launch, enticing folks to plan a visit a month ahead, and you're only shelling out five bucks a day. Then, as you hit the three-week mark, you could bump that up to twenty bucks daily. And when you're two weeks away, consider going for 50 bucks a day.

The key? Do the math and double-check your figures. It's crucial to avoid overspending based on your budget. Meta's ad system works on daily budgets, so you'll need to divide your desired budget by the number of days your ads will run. Also, factor in where and when you want to allocate funds, plus the number of ad variations you have.

When it comes to ad images, our findings show that the ones resonating the most are those capturing the essence of a Sunday service experience. That's why it's wise to stock up on content before you launch. My suggestion: about a month prior, organize a worship night and hire a photographer to capture high-quality shots. These images can be gold when you're promoting your grand opening.

Videos

As I am writing this book, vertical video rules the roost. You want your ads to blend seamlessly with social media trends. So, opt for vertical recordings, not horizontal. Steer clear of the commercial-style vibe – avoid the look of church announcements with fancy graphics and jingles.

Another trick to make your ads less ad-like? No need for a fancy camera. Your smartphone will do just fine. Have your lead pastor stand outside the venue, where your congregation will gather, and deliver a message. Here's the script you can use.

Option 1:

"Something NEW is coming to [CITY NAME] and You're Invited to be a part! My name is [NAME] and I'm the

Lead Pastor of [CHURCH NAME]! A Brand new, life-giving church coming to [CITY NAME] on [LAUNCH DAY].

I want to personally invite you to our Grand opening. We'll have uplifting worship music, an encouraging word from the Bible, and tons of fun things for the kids.

On [LAUNCH DAY + TIME] at [ADDRESS / MEETING LOCATION]

Plan your visit below and we'll see you there!"

Option 2:

"Hey [CITY NAME]! This video could change your life!

Well, kind of...

My name is [NAME] and I'm the Lead Pastor of [CHURCH NAME]! A Brand new, life-giving church coming to [CITY NAME] on [LAUNCH DAY].

I want to personally invite you to our Grand opening. We'll have uplifting worship music, an encouraging word from the Bible, and tons of fun things for the kids.

On [LAUNCH DAY + TIME] at [ADDRESS / MEETING LOCATION]

Plan your visit below and we'll see you there!"

At ChurchCandy, our guiding principle is 'mission over method.' Depending on your budget, you can decide how many variations you should craft. And remember, it doesn't have to be just you in the videos. Involve your spouse, other team leaders – they can all contribute and be part of the message. However, for your grand opening, I suggest that the lead pastor take center stage in most of the content. That's just my two cents.

You can also tap into popular sounds. For Instagram Reels, compile b-roll or snapshots from past events – worship nights, pre-service or pre-launch gatherings – and set them to music. Add a text overlay that reads, 'Hey there! [City], you're invited to our grand opening. Check out the details in the caption!' This approach engages and intrigues, luring them into reading the caption. And in that caption – the main text of your ad – lay out the launch details.

Here are a few ad Screenshots that have proven effective for us. But, remember, ads evolve monthly, so what works for us might not be the magic formula for you by the time you read this book.

Vibrant Church
Sponsored · ⊕   ✕ ⋮

Hey Montgomery Area! Are you looking for your place, your people, and your purpose? We are starting a new church just for you!

Hey, my name is Michael. My wife Carmen and I are the lead pastors of Vibrant Church. We want to personally invite you to our brand NEW CAMPUS in Montgomery on August 6th.

At Vibrant we believe it's our mission to help people find focus for living.

Our kids team is ready for little ones. We believe that kids should have a blast at church every single week - and at Vibrant Church, we make this a priority.

We're excited to celebrate with you!

Join us at 1701 McCaleb Rd, Montgomery, TX 77316

Tap to RSVP! 🎉

FORM ON FACEBOOK
You're Invited to Our Grand Opening! [This Sunday]   Learn more

 Vivid Church
Sponsored · ⊕   ✕ ⋮

Hey Orange County Area! You don't have to live this life alone 🙂

Hey! My name is Joe, my wife, Krissy, and I are the Pastors of Vivid Church! A new life giving church in Brea. We would like to invite you to join us on for our Grand Opening on Sunday, August 11th!

There will be activities for the kids, a life-giving word, new friends, and amazing worship! So come hang out and make some new friends!

Our address is 562 E Lambert Rd, Brea, CA 92821

We can't wait to meet you, click the link below and we will see you soon! 🙌

FORM ON FACEBOOK
Grand Opening | New Church in Orange County   Learn more

Like I mentioned, we're all about mission over method. My team's always brainstorming new ideas, and we regularly switch gears when something works. Over time, ads can get a bit tired, which we call 'ad fatigue' in the biz. That's when we infuse fresh content to perk things up.

So go ahead, borrow these ideas, adapt them – just be aware of the risks. If you're up for it, you can even copy-paste this stuff. But, a word of caution: it's at your own risk because it is different for everyone. Now, if you're feeling the need for a smoother journey, consider hiring us. At ChurchCandy, we specialize in setting up and managing all of this for you. We're on a mission to connect 1 million people to local churches. At the time of writing this book, we've already connected over 120,000 people to over 500 local churches. We've got the know-how to pack your grand opening service, and have helped hundreds of church planters do this already. You can scan this QR code or go to church-candy.com/churchplant to hear some of their stories.

churchcandy.com/church-plant

POST LAUNCH:
HOW TO GET NEW GUESTS
EVERY SUNDAY

CHAPTER 10

YOUR CHURCH WEBSITE

Once you're meeting every week and the excitement from your grand opening has settled down, it's time to make your landing page into a great website.

Your church's website should accomplish 3 things:

First, it should be an open invitation. Remember, your website isn't just for the people who already come to your church; it's a way to welcome new visitors. When you build your website, make sure to keep this in mind. That big, bold button on your homepage, right at the top, should be a warm invitation. It's like saying, "Hey there! Come check us out and plan a visit!"

Second, your website needs to share information clearly and easily. I've seen a lot of church websites that make it hard to find simple things, like where they're located. Your website should be like an open book, giving all the details a guest might need. This means having a clear address on the homepage and a 'Plan Your Visit' page that's easy to find and helps newcomers feel welcome.

And finally, your website should be full of inspiration, like confetti at a celebration. Your church isn't just a place; it's a home full of love, faith, and community. Your website should feel as warm as your Sunday sermons. Wondering what pages every church website should have? It's like a checklist: 'Plan Your Visit,' 'About Us,' 'Giving,' 'Next-Gen Ministries,' and more. You can have separate pages for children's and student ministries if you want, but it's not necessary. You'll also want to keep in mind that your 'Staff' page typically one of the highest visited pages of any church website.

Let's dive deeper into the 'Plan Your Visit' page. This little gem should be your go-to landing pad for any web ads you're running. If you're tinkering with Google ads or similar, steer clear of the church's main page; send them here instead.

Here's the recipe for an A+ 'Plan Your Visit' page:

1. VIP Treatment Form: Let folks snag that VIP experience – a freebie, a warm welcome, a first-class intro to your church if they plan

their visit online. It's not just a sweet deal; it's a golden opportunity to connect and make sure they have a stellar first experience, even before they walk through the church doors.

2. Set Expectations: Give them the lowdown on what to expect. How long are services? What's the dress code? What's the deal with kids' ministry? Any FAQs that folks new to church might ponder should be answered right here. Walk them through the journey: you start with some toe-tapping worship, followed by a message of encouragement from the pastor, and then comes the chance to mingle in the lobby before and after service.

3. Life-Changing Testimonials: Sprinkle in some video or written testimonials from folks whose lives have been transformed in your church. It's the social proof served on a silver platter – real stories, real experiences, and a tad more believable than just hearing it from the lead pastor or staff.

Your church's website is the front door to your church. Make sure to use real pictures of people smiling all throughout your website (no stock photos). And make sure your Address and services times are easily accessible near the top of the home page, and on your website footer. Adding this information to the footer is important, because it'll automatically be on every page of your website.

Having a solid website is the foundation to a strong online footprint. But a good website doesn't mean anything if you don't show up when people search for you. In the next chapter, we'll dive into Search Engine Optimization. We'll talk all about how to make your website actually show up on Google when people search things like "churches near me" or "churches in [your city name]".

CHAPTER 11

SEO

Have you ever pulled up the Google page and typed 'restaurants near me'? Of course you have. We all have! Well, in this chapter I'm going to tell you the basics of SEO and how to make your church show up at the top of the page whenever someone searches 'churches near me' on Google.

But first, some context and definitions. SEO stands for search engine optimization. This is the process in which you build an online digital footprint large enough to where Google recognizes that your ministry not only exists, but is legitimate enough to recommend to users looking for churches in their area online.

SEO can sometimes feel like the least thrilling growth strategy in the bunch, mainly because it lacks the immediate adrenaline rush of some of its counterparts.

It's a bit like comparing investing to the stock market. I've got pals who dive headfirst into day trading, flipping Tesla stocks, Disney shares, and the Apple pie, hoping to hit the jackpot in their spare time. But truth be told, at a certain point, it's no longer investing; it's closer to gambling. Especially when you consider the steady and proven growth of a trusty index fund or mutual fund, chugging along at a respectable 10% year over year. Not flashy, but reliable.

SEO shares this same kind of steadfast consistency.

With ads, you can see rapid returns on your investment. You flick the switch on a Facebook ad come Monday, and by Sunday, new families might already be knocking on your church doors. The catch with ads, though, is that you're continually forking over cash for them to keep working. Once you stop the payments, the visitors tend to stop... well... visiting.

People say SEO is similar to buying a house, while paid ads are more like renting. Renting was a breeze when I first graduated from college – quick move-in, paperwork, and a deposit, and I was good to go. Plus, it was light on the wallet; no hefty down payments or worries about maintenance costs and the like that homeowners have to deal with.

On the flip side, buying our home was a more complicated process. We had to secure bank approval, save up for a sizable down payment, and jump through some somewhat ridiculous hoops. But the reason we went through it all? We were investing for the long haul of life. And that's the beauty of investing in a well-thought-out SEO strategy – it's evergreen.

Turn off your ads, and your influx of new guests dries up. SEO, on the other hand, is like preparing a grand feast for visitors that keeps on coming, provided you have space in your church for them. Once you start ranking for keywords like '(city name) churches', 'non-denominational churches in (city name)', or 'churches near me,' you'd better be ready for the influx.

Sure, Google's algorithm is a shapeshifter, constantly evolving. A decade from now, the strategies we employ to climb those rankings will likely be vastly different. So, instead of inundating you with fleeting hacks and short-term tricks, I'm going to lay out some timeless fundamentals. These should remain rock-solid unless Google decides to pack its bags and retire, but I don't foresee AI or chatbots replacing Google's search prowess anytime soon.

Google Business Profile

Your Google business profile is essentially your online storefront on Google Maps. It prominently showcases reviews, your physical address, a brief description, and often, a few preview photos. It even offers the nifty feature of allowing you to post content.

What's fascinating, though, is our discovery that a staggering 90% of web traffic stemming from Google searches doesn't arrive directly at your website's doorstep. Instead, it first stops by at your Google business profile, which then acts as a signpost directing visitors to your website.

This is even something that I, personally, tend to follow. When I'm on the hunt for a restaurant, I typically turn to a Google business profile. I use the Google Maps app on my phone to scan reviews, pinpoint the location, and hopefully, get a visual taste of the place through photos. And guess what? Churches aren't exempt from this.

So, given 90% of your web traffic passes through your Google Business Profile, it's paramount that your SEO strategy leans more towards enhancing the ranking of your Google Business Profile rather than fixating solely on elevating your website's position. Mind you, these two aspects are tightly intertwined. Generally, when your website climbs higher in rankings, your Google business profile follows suit, and vice versa.

Your primary aim with your Google business profile should be to secure a spot in what we affectionately term the "three-pack." These are the prestigious top three Google Maps listings that pop up when folks search for local keywords.

So, with these concepts in mind, here are some fundamental steps you can take to give your Google business profile a boost:

Accumulate Google Reviews

Yes, it might sound unconventional for a church to actively seek Google reviews. I'm aware that comedians like John Crist have found humor in the idea of reviews on Google about churches, but, as quirky as it might seem, if you aim to expand your online reach and ensure that people locate you via Google, having reviews is important. In this case, more is indeed merrier. However, don't flood your entire contact list with review requests all at once. Instead, opt for a "drip campaign."

This approach entails reaching out to 10 to 20 individuals per week over time. If you amass hundreds of reviews in a single day, Google may flag your account and remove those reviews, suspecting they're fake, paid for, or even fraudulent.

So, concentrate on getting Google reviews. If you can formulate a strategy to consistently gather these reviews, you're good to go. An easy trick you can employ in Planning Center is to set a timer for two weeks after someone starts contributing financially. After this period, send them a review request, politely asking for their feedback and including a link to your Google business profile.

Also, your profile's description shouldn't just mirror your mission statement. It's essential that your description incorporates relevant search terms that users might employ when searching on Google. This way, Google recognizes that your church is pertinent to their search.

Here's an example:

"Vibrant Church is a life giving spirit filled church in the north Houston area. One church in 2 locations in The Woodlands and Montgomery. Pastors Michael and Carmen Scobey planted the church in The Wood-lands with the goal of helping people discover authentic community, passionate faith, and a life of calling and

fulfillment in Montgomery County. Real people with a real passion to live Vibrant life in Jesus!"

Now, you might be pondering, "Brady, this text sounds a bit quirky." Well, you're absolutely correct; it does have a whimsical twist. Feel at ease to tailor it to your liking and employ your own wordsmith skills. What's key here is that it conveys crucial information. Take note of how it strategically drops terms like your church's denomination, church name, city name, and more.

Moving on to the visual aspect, your description isn't the only star of the show. You also need a collection of top-tier photos. Just as you've meticulously curated your social media profile, your Google business profile deserves that same attention and care. These images should paint a vivid picture of what a typical Sunday experience entails for the average visitor to your church.

Picture this: cheerful faces, warm interactions, welcoming gestures extended to guests, the congregation immersed in worship, and your lead pastor delivering an inspiring sermon from the pulpit. Every single one of these images should find its place on your Google business profile.

Now, about frequency – on a monthly basis, consider adding two to three additional photos to your Google business profile. It's like tending to a digital garden; it needs regular nurturing. To excel in the realm of Google, you've got to align with their preferences. And guess what? They're fond of businesses that actively engage with their platform. It's like showing up to the party; even if you don't talk to everyone, just being there earns you some of those much coveted brownie points. Your increased activity on your Google Business Profile can earn you favor in search rankings.

Here's a duo of strategies to achieve this:

1. **The Effortless Route:** Anytime you're prepping a post for Facebook or Instagram, go ahead and share it simultaneously on your Google business profile. This straightforward method is easy to scale and doesn't demand extra effort.
2. **Strategic Content Creation:** Craft posts that are specifically tailored to keywords that people might be using in their searches. This more intentional approach can enhance your profile's performance in Google's eyes.

Ok, now let's take a few minutes to dive into some other aspects, like exploring what insights the Bible has to offer regarding the specific needs and concerns of individuals.

Ensuring a steady influx of reviews on your Google business profile while maintaining a regular posting schedule is a recipe for enhancing your search rankings gradually. Additionally, it's essential to embed your Google business profile seamlessly into your website. This brings us to the next step, which is making sure your church's website is easy to find on search engines.

Step one involves infusing your website with ample amounts of high quality written content. This content should mirror the keywords people typically employ in their searches. Like the description on your Google business profile, your website copy needs to resonate with these search terms.

While incorporating images into your website is crucial, it's paramount that these images aren't generic stock photos. Instead, opt for genuine photographs featuring members of your congregation. The same principles apply here—smiling faces, warm interactions, hospitality extended to visitors, enthusiastic worship, and snapshots of your sermons in action.

Now, let's reveal a surefire strategy to ascend the ranks of Google listings: garnering backlinks from other websites. Amidst all the algorithm tweaks over the years, this tactic remains a steadfast route to success—getting high-authority websites to link back to your church's website.

Here are a couple of tactics to achieve this:

1. **Forge partnerships** with local news outlets and newspapers. While it's true that traditional newspapers aren't as widely read these days, and local news viewership might have dwindled in recent years, there's still an opportunity. When they cover a story about your church, politely request that they include a link to your website in the online article. This can be particularly effective if you're gearing up for a grand opening event, which could attract media attention. You can also reach out to journalists who specialize in covering local events via Instagram direct messages.

2. **Enroll in your local chamber of commerce.** Many local chambers maintain directories on their websites, which can link back to your church's site.

3. **Ensure your presence** on various online local directories like Nextdoor and Yelp. These

listings contribute to bolstering your website's ranking.

Lastly, when you organize significant events and manage to secure publicity and press coverage, capitalize on this opportunity to generate backlinks. Encourage local news articles to include links to your website, as this practice will gradually enhance your site's ranking over time.

CHAPTER 12

THE PLAN YOUR VISIT FUNNEL

If you are anything like me, this is the chapter you've been waiting for.

Welcome to the world of Facebook and Instagram ads – your golden ticket to having fresh faces at your church doorstep every single Sunday!

Now, hold on a sec! If you're thinking, "Hey, my church isn't exactly a newborn seedling anymore, my grand opening is years behind me," no worries! Stick around because this chapter is still packed with gold nuggets that'll get those guest numbers soaring on a regular basis.

In earlier chapters, we talked about crafting Facebook ads for your launch team's growth, whipping up a buzz for an interest party, locking in those cozy pastor-coffee chats, or getting folks excited about your grand opening service, so this chapter might sound like a familiar tune, but don't change the channel just yet! We're sprinkling some extra magic here, tailor-made for roping in those new guests to join you for Sunday service.

Imagine this as your launching pad: a sales funnel. Businesses that thrive have been using these for ages, and honestly, I believe the Church could totally level up by embracing them, too. This is like the key piece of the grand puzzle – the one-stop-shop for your Plan Your Visit strategy.

This funnel starts wide at the top and gradually tapers down to a snug little passage at the base, like a mega-catching net. So, your ad grabs everyone's attention and they're like, "Whoa, what's this?" They all step into the wide part of the funnel, then some people, the curious clickers, they're intrigued by your ad and they tap on it. They are headed to your landing page, a sort of mid-funnel stop.

But wait, it gets even narrower. The real-deal enthusiasts, they fill out a form saying, "Hey, I'm dropping by your church!" That's another step down the funnel, a smaller gate to pass through. And ta-da, at the itty-bitty opening at the bottom? Those are the folks who've made it – they're in the pews, checking out your church real and in person. It's like the funnel sifts through the crowd, finding you the people who are the best fit for your church.

At ChurchCandy, we call this the Plan Your Visit funnel. Can you catch the distinction here? It's not about just slapping on some branding or chasing engagement just for the sake of it. Nope, this is a whole different ball game. But what is the start of the funnel? That's all about sparking engagement, but with a purpose – to nudge people right into the funnel itself. Think of it like opening a door for them.

You can't expect people to leap from seeing an ad to becoming church regulars in one swift move. That's like skipping steps on a ladder – it hardly ever pans out. You need to guide them through a sales funnel. When this marketing dance is done right, it's like laying out a clear map for them one step at a time.

Our Plan Your Visit funnel is like a magical conveyor belt. It takes people from just being passive onlookers to raising their hand and saying, "I'm visiting!" Then, bam, they're inside the church. This funnel is like the master choreographer, leading the dance step by step. That's what direct response marketing does – it offers up the next move they need to make.

Imagine a garden hose. An intact one is like a funnel – you know water goes in at one end and out at the other. No fuss, no detours. But now picture a hose with a leak in it – uh-oh. Suddenly, there are no promises. Water might go in, but who knows if it'll come out on the other side? Same deal with chasing engagement. You might pour in time and money, amazing content and ads, but the returns might not flow back as expected. It's like patching up that hose – fixing the leaks means a smoother flow and results that make a splash.

Here's a little scenario: imagine someone strolls by and gives your Facebook post a thumbs-up. But then, poof, they vanish into the digital abyss. That engagement hit a dead end because, well, you didn't lay down the breadcrumbs for the next step. You're sort of expecting them to be mind readers, to just follow along. But guess what? They needed a nudge, a sales funnel to help guide them.

Speaking from my own turf as someone who battles undiagnosed ADHD on a daily basis – I'm all about those next steps. If I'm left hanging without a clear direction, my focus takes a nosedive, and my task disappears into thin air. On the flip side, if I'm smothered with too many instructions, I freeze up like an overloaded computer. All I need is that one, simple (and single) next step in the process.

Now, here's a nugget: you might be way ahead on this funnel thing without even realizing it. Think about it – you're taking folks who feel a bit lost and introducing them to Jesus. Picture yourself on stage, preaching your heart out. When the altar call rings out, you don't just leave it at "Who wants to embrace Jesus?" You give them the roadmap for the next steps.

If you're not a fan of having a stagnant crew in your church, listen up – you've got to serve up those next steps for spiritual growth. You've probably crossed paths with Brady Shearer, the brain behind Pro Church Tools. He's all about church branding and social media. Here's a gem I picked up from him: growing your church isn't just about headcount. Nope, it's about tracking the next moves, too.

It's important to keep track of how many people take a "next-step" in their relationship with God. Tracking salvation is key. And don't forget about another important thing to track – baptisms. How many people has your church baptized this year? Also, keep an eye on those in your growth track, membership class, or life groups. These are all important next steps, too. Discipleship is just helping people take a "next-step" in their relationship with God.

Now, let's rewind a bit. Before anyone ever knows Christ, gets baptized, or even thinks about joining your church, there's a small but essential step they each have to take. They've got to first walk into your church building. They need that firsthand experience. And that's where the Plan Your Visit funnel shines like a superstar. It's your ticket to getting them through your doors, and from there, you lead them onward through the journey of their relationship with God.

Alright, funnel time. You've grasped the concept, now let's dive into how to wield it like a champ to fill those church pews. Here's a peek at some real-life digits from one of our clients who leads a church in Wisconsin.

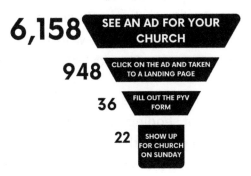

They spent $331.90 on ads and had 6,158 people see them on Facebook and Instagram. From there, 948 people clicked on the ads and were taken to the landing page that had a Plan Your Visit form on it. Then 36 people took the time to fill out the form. Finally, 22 families showed up to their Sunday service.

Behold the magic of the Plan Your Visit strategy in full swing! They only shelled out $15 per family that stepped through their church doors. And that doesn't even account for those who had a visit in their plans but couldn't make it – they might just pop by on another Sunday.

Now that you're in sync with the potency of a sales funnel, let me introduce you to Russel Brunson. This guy practically put sales funnels on the map and co-founded ClickFunnels, a software haven for marketers. He's basically the guy who wrote the book – well, a whole series of books, actually, on the topic.

Russel's ace move? He waved the banner for landing pages instead of sending traffic straight to your website. A clean-cut page with a crystal-clear call to action. It's like giving your audience a golden ticket. Unlike your church's website, which might be bursting with tabs and info, this landing page is a clean breeze.

Your church's website – probably loaded with all sorts of info, tabs, and chats about what your church does – is something that a newcomer could easily feel lost in the shuffle of. And that's where the landing page swoops in to save the day.

Lucky for us, killer software is up for grabs to whip up those landing pages and keep things shipshape. And guess what? Facebook ads tie the whole enchilada together. No need to tweak your website – the form is hosted directly on Facebook.

Sales funnels have made businesses rake in millions. It's like a savvy worldly tactic we can flip for the greater good. A Plan Your Visit funnel? Brace yourself, because that's the potential to welcome 20-50 new families to your church each month. Just let that sink in – talk about a Kingdom-sized impact!

What does a Plan Your Visit funnel look like?

The first step in the Plan Your Visit funnel calls for an opt-in page. Here's the scoop – you give them a sneak peek of what to expect during their visit, and then open up the floor for them to fill out a form, planning their visit ahead. Something like, "Give us the scoop, we're excited to see you!"

Have a look at how Vibrant Church does it at vibranthtx.com/plan-your-visit.

Now, moving on to step two in the funnel – the Thank You page. This little beauty pops up right after they hit that submit button. But it's not just a polite nod – it's your chance to serve up the next set of moves.

Check out Vibrant Church's Thank You page at vibranthtx.com/thank-you-page.

But hold on a second, the sparkle of those pages will fade if no one is there to lay eyes on them. And if you're not sure how to follow up with those form-fillers, well, no worries – I've covered that for you in Chapter 7. But let's cap off this chapter by diving into how to get that Plan Your Visit Funnel in front of folks who happen to be scouting for a church.

Now, heads up, this topic is vast and we're just scratching the surface. But for now, let's talk about what's worked like a charm for us in speeding up those PYVs (that's someone all set to visit your church) – Facebook and Instagram ads.

Why Run Ads on Facebook for Your Church?

Tapping into Facebook ads is like snagging low-hanging fruit – it's straightforward and wallet-friendly, making their way like a beeline to your local community. Facebook boasts a whopping 2.91 billion monthly active users, and Instagram's not far behind with around 1 billion folks hanging out there, too. The best part is our clients are only dishing out about $15 to score 1000 views with their ads, on average.

That means as long as you're armed with a solid plan and a surefire way to reel in a return on your investment (which, guess what, I'm unraveling for you right here in this book), using Facebook ads to lure new families to your church is practically a no-brainer at this point.

When it comes to your Facebook ad game plan, keep it laser-focused: the bullseye is getting families geared up to plan a visit to your Sunday service. Hey, don't get me wrong, you can definitely flaunt ads for events or specific sermon series if you want. But the golden nugget here? The call to action, the nudge for the next step – it should be all about "plan your visit."

Now, before we dive into the deep end of our Plan Your Visit Facebook ads strategy in the next chapter, there's a little something you need: a killer video to feature in your ads.

What to put in your Plan Your Visit video ad

A super effective way to draw families into planning a visit? Video ads, hands down. Now, there's a million approaches to this, but here's a gem: the simplest selfie-style videos are golden, based on our experience. Your lead pastor just chatting away right into their phone. Now, you might be itching to whip out your fancy camera gear you use for live streams, but here's why you shouldn't – this isn't about being an ad. You want it to blend in like regular Facebook content. So, give your phone its moment to shine.

Hold it tall and proud, and make sure you're in a well-lit area. If you can, stand outside the church – it's like a visual breadcrumb to your location. But if that doesn't work, hit up a local park or a spot near your church that everyone knows. It's all about familiar territory.

Solid-color walls? Not your best bet. More depth in the background is a visual winner. People watching should get that urge to be right where you are, so choose your backdrop wisely.

Now, the golden rule – they've got to hear you loud and clear. If the wind's making a fuss outside, pop on a lavalier lapel mic, plugged straight into your phone, and once you've got the audio down pat, resist the urge to go all Hollywood on the video. No major edits, no background music, no logo popping up in the corner. This isn't your cue to be fancy, it's not an ad, remember?

Oh, and don't forget – your communication is more than just words. Your expressions and body language, they are your co-stars. Flash those pearly whites, radiate excitement like you just won a prize, and imagine you're welcoming a visitor to your church. Put that warmth and kindness into your voice and expressions. Win them over with genuineness and sincerity.

So, once you've nailed down your spot, locked in good lighting, and confirmed the audio's crystal clear, roll the camera. But what's the script, you ask? Well, I've got some successful lines from my church to share – and feel free to borrow them for yours!

Video Script for your Plan Your Visit ad

Here's a sample script. You can personalize it by inserting your church's information in the brackets:

Hey, {Houston}. This is {Pastor Brady} and I want to personally invite you to our church this Sunday.

Here you'll find a welcoming community, uplifting worship, and an encouraging message about Jesus.

{We're real people with a real passion to live a vibrant life in Jesus.}

We're located {right in the heart of The Woodlands next to the mall and pavilion.}

Plan your visit below and get a free gift when you arrive!

We'll see you at {10:00 am!} Have a blessed day.

It only takes 5 to 7 sentences to introduce yourself, your church, to lay out your mission, and to drop a pin on your location. And then comes the magic – the invitation, followed by your clear-cut next step. It's simple, but trust me, the impact is massive.

Want a sneak peek at how this plays out? Head over to our site where you can see examples of how this works: churchcandy.com/pyv-videos.

Remember when I said "hands off the editing"? Well, there's one little tweak I'd recommend. About 80% of Facebook videos are enjoyed without sound. So, adding captions is a smart move. There are a bunch of ways to do this, but I personally like the Instagram app. If your video's under 60 seconds, you can whip up an Instagram reel. Here's the trick: add captions before posting, then save the file right back onto your phone to use elsewhere, also.

Texts to Accompany your Plan Your Visit Ad

You're going to want some text to accompany your Plan Your Visit video when you post it. Keep in mind, these are specifically for ads aimed at encouraging viewers to plan a visit. I'd advise against using these for the longer, inspirational video ads.

When crafting our ads, we break them down into two parts: the hook and the body. Usually, the hook shifts while the body remains consistent across different ads. While they may be a tad longer, I've found that longer ads tend to attract more attention and yield higher show rates.

Here are some examples of different hooks:

*Hey {TOWN} Area! *waving hand emoji**

Are you looking for a life-giving church in the {TOWN} area? A place to really call home and belong?

This last one is a bit longer and has a little different angle, but it does still tend to

work well.

The Bible says that God didn't make you to do life alone.

And the technology we have in 2024 is great for connecting with others, but why are so many people lonelier than ever? Why are depression rates at an all-time high?

I believe the solution isn't on your smartphone, but it's through a relationship with Jesus and getting plugged into a life-giving community.

Notice how most of these call out the local area? You should test out different hooks at the beginning of your ads, but you can leave the body the same.

Here's an example of a good body text:

Hi, my name is {NAME}. My wife, {SPOUSE NAME}, and I are the lead pastors here at {CHURCH NAME} in {TOWN}.

I want to personally invite you and your family to join us this Sunday for church at {SERVICE TIMES}.

We are a new, life-giving, church that {MISSION STATEMENT}

Our kids' team is ready for little ones. We believe that kids should have a blast at church - and at {CHURCH NAME} we make this a priority. Our vision for Children's ministry is that your kids would have fun while learning about Jesus!

When you plan your visit below, we'll roll out the red carpet and you'll get the VIP treatment when you visit! (or) *When you plan your visit below, you'll get a free gift when you come visit!*

We cannot wait to meet you, so plan your visit below and we'll see you Sunday at {SERVICE TIMES}!

PS: we are located at {LOCATION INFO}

Good headlines we use are:

Plan Your Visit to Vibrant Church

We're Saving Your Seat on Sunday

[NEW] Life-Giving Church in The Woodlands

The last one will literally have the word *NEW* in all caps and brackets. If you're a church plant, make that word shine – embrace it confidently. Remember, you're the fresh face compared to those giants that have been around for decades.

Now, as you piece together your ads, let your devotion be to a mission, not just a method. The mission here? To guide new families into planning a visit. Don't hesitate to tweak the wording and test out various versions.

See how this stands out from the crowd that's just chasing engagement? Notice the crystal-clear call to action? This, my friend, is prime direct response advertising in action. And I hope the puzzle pieces are starting to snap into place for you.

With your video and text all set, you're good to roll in some traffic to your Plan Your Visit funnel!

Our META Ads Shotgun Method: *Save Money by Making More Ads!*

One of the most common questions pastors ask me is how much they're going to spend on getting a new family in their church. Over time I've learned to follow Jesus' example and return a question with a question. So, when someone asks, "How much should I spend on ads?" I respond with, "Well, what's your goal?" Next, I break it down clearly – knowing your target upfront makes the whole hitting-the-mark thing more of a breeze. Before you pull the trigger, you've got to have your aim locked in place!

Hold tight, though, as we'll circle back to numbers and goals by the end of this chapter. I've first got a gem to share with you that'll tackle those tough questions. But first, let's chat about this aiming and shooting business. This brings us to a big-time principle – enter the Shotgun Method briefly mentioned previously.

Now, I'm a good ol' Texas boy who used to tag along with my grandpa for hunting trips. If I was gearing up for a hunt, I wouldn't pack a rifle – I'd go for the shotgun. Rifles wouldn't be your go-to (unless your skills exceed mine) for duck hunting or skeet shooting. A rifle fires off just one round at a time. So, you've got to be dead-on with your aim for that single round to strike the target.

But here's where the shotgun shines – it sends out a cluster of tiny pellets in a single shot. That boosts your odds of nailing a flying duck. Every trigger pull throws a dozen chances your way to hit the mark. And trust me, a dozen trumps one, every single time!

Now, my grandpa might raise an eyebrow knowing his hunting lessons primed me for running a marketing ministry. But hey, they still did the trick! When I'm cranking out Facebook ads for churches, I'm all about the Shotgun Method. I whip up a bunch of ads and let 'em loose on the internet.

Ever heard of a split test? It's like comparing two different email subject lines or website landing pages for your Facebook ads. You run a small experiment, see which one works

 better, and then channel your budget into the winner. Well, the Shotgun Method is like split testing on steroids! Let me give you an example from one of my clients:

I cooked up a whopping 42 versions of Plan Your Visit ads for a church. Each one was a blend of different media like images, videos, and slideshows, along with a twist of text and headlines. And guess what? These ads weren't just floating around solo. We're talking 8 different placements across platforms like Facebook mobile feed, Instagram feed, Facebook desktop feed, and more. So, that's not one ad, not 8 ads, but a grand total of 336 unique ad variations. But these weren't all wildly distinct. Nope, I simply tinkered with the key components that mattered most.

Keep your eyes on the prize – the headline and that very first line of text pack a punch with your audience. Getting these spot-on is more than half the battle for a winning ad. Believe it or not, the secret lies in those high-impact areas – roughly 80% of our shotgun split test results come from finessing those tiny but ever so mighty details. That's why we channel a bunch of energy into these parts, testing different phrases and words to see what's click-worthy.

When you fling out 300+ versions of your Plan Your Visit ad, you become a pro at spotting what clicks within your community. After giving these ads a spin for about a week, you roll up your sleeves and crunch the numbers, figuring out which ones to pull the plug on and which ones deserve an encore performance.

People always raise their eyebrows when I use the often-disputed mantra of "quantity over quality." But here's the real-world proof. If you were out duck hunting, would you bet it all on one perfect bullet? Or would you rather pepper the sky with over 300 decent bullets each time? Which strategy would up your odds of enjoying duck for dinner?

Likewise, instead of just backing one video, you're scattering dozens, if not hundreds, of different videos out there and waiting to see which ones strike gold. And guess what? You're seriously boosting your odds of having new faces grace your church next Sunday because of the more advanced exposure.

But before we dive into the nuts and bolts of the Shotgun Method, here are a couple of things to think about. You've got to nail down a campaign objective and figure out your target audience for the campaign.

Campaign Objectives

You've got three choices when it comes to optimizing your ads: conversions, traffic, or lead generation. Let's break it down:

1. **Conversions:** Here, you're sending traffic over to your website or landing page, and then you're keeping tabs on where users venture

next. Facebook does the legwork, counting how many people hit that "Plan Your Visit" form. Sure, there's Facebook's tracking pixel to help, but honestly, from my experience, setting it up's a bit of a headache and it's not the most accurate. Now, since iOS 14 dropped from Apple, conversion ads took a bit of a hit – they're not as effective.

2. **Traffic:** If your campaign's all about traffic, your aim is to ferry as many people as possible to your website's landing page. But hold up, you're not watching what they do once they're there – you're simply racking up a headcount of visitors.

3. **Lead Generation:** This one is a favorite among most of our clients – they're snagging over 30 families to plan a visit each month with this. The trick here is guiding traffic to a landing page right on Facebook. This page packs a form, with the user's name, email, and phone number conveniently filled in.

Here's the cool part – you can toss in a question for the user to answer manually. Like, ask them how they stumbled upon your church or which service they're eyeing. Writing an answer requires a tad more effort from the lead than just tapping buttons. But it reels the person in, making them feel like they're part of the process, setting off that mental spark of "I'm filling out a form, and this church is about to hit me up."

And here's the cherry on top – this route is the budget-friendly pick. You're keeping Facebook and Instagram users right in their app haven. Those platforms are all about keeping their users in-house, rather than shipping 'em off to a separate website.

Targeting

With your objective in the bag, the next step is locking in your ad's audience. My advice? Kick off with a pretty expansive group – think people ages 25 to 60, both men and women, within a 30-mile radius of the church. Back in the day, Facebook let you target based on "Christians" interests, but we never quite dove into that. Trust me, zooming in too tight on interests could crank up your ad expenses quite a bit. Our sweet spot for top results? Kickstarting with a broader audience.

Use that wide audience to determine which ads are the most effective. Then you can test the best ads across more specific demographics:

- Parents with children 0-18 years old
- Married couples
- Recently moved
- Women only
- Men Only

The Shotgun Method in Action

Now that you've decided on your campaign objective and target audience, we'll look at the Shotgun Method in action. I'll start with an illustration that simplifies these marketing terms and explain this method more clearly.

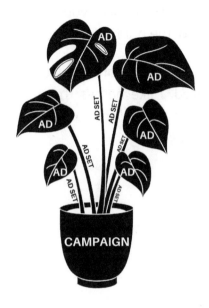

Imagine a potted plant where the campaign is the pot, the ad sets are the stems, and the ads are the leaves. The campaign is where you control the main objective of the ads (conversions, traffic, or lead generations). The ad set is where you control the targeting and placement (who is seeing the ads and where are they seeing them). The ads themselves are obviously what people actually see on Facebook and Instagram.

I know the math can seem overwhelming, but stay with me because the outcome is worth it. When you start building your campaign, you just want one ad set with one ad. So, the pot has one stem and one leaf.

We'll give that ad set a name so we can keep everything organized. I like names that describe exactly what's inside of them: for example, *Collage Image - Headline 1 - Hook 1.*

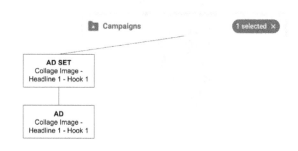

While you can nest multiple ads within an ad set, the Shotgun Method keeps it simple – one ad per ad set. By fixing the budget at the ad set level, every ad enjoys an equal share of the spotlight.

Now, with your initial ad set shaped up, targets locked in, placements dialed, and design slick, the next move is copying the entire ad set. Think of it like planting another stem and leaf in your potted plant. Boom, you've got two identical ad sets, each boasting clones of the same ads. This is where you introduce a twist to the new ad set and ad – just one variable gets the switcheroo. In the demo, for instance, Hook 1 morphs into Hook 2. Everything else in the ad and ad set remains an exact replica.

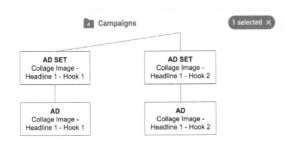

You can duplicate the ad set one more time and update the hook to hook 3. Now you have 3 different variations, testing different hooks. You could stop here, but this is just the first step.

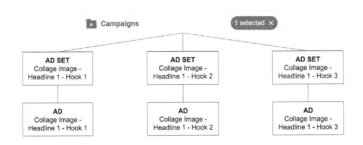

Now you will select all 3 of these ad sets, duplicate them, and then change another variable. In the example below, you'll see that I just changed from headline 1 to Headline 2. Everything else stayed the same.

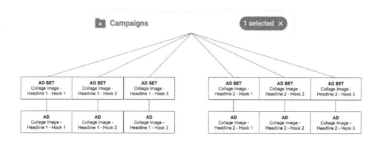

Next, just rinse and repeat as you continue multiplying ad sets, changing one part of the ad each time.

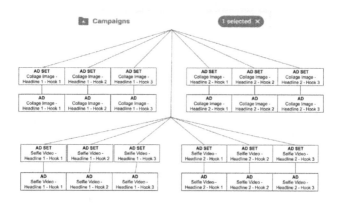

You'll keep doing this until you successfully create ads using all of the assets you prepared. It's not uncommon for us to use more than 12+ variations here.

Scaling The Shotgun Method

After I've set everything up, I keep those ads running for a solid 10 days before I even think about tweaks. Often, we'll start seeing people planning visits within the first 24 hours of the ad launch. After that initial period, at the 10-day mark, it's time to dim the lights on the underperformers and crank up the spotlight on the rockstars.

The winners in the ad game? Oh, they get a duplicate ticket. We whip up fresh variations of these top-performing ads – same ad content, different target audience. Sometimes we'll do a straight-up clone job and let both ad sets run simultaneously, no changes made whatsoever. It's all about increasing the budget for an ad that's already proven its worth.

The Shotgun Method isn't just a flash in the pan. It's a long-haul game plan that goes beyond throwing up a post and crossing your fingers for Sunday's turnout. This isn't about a quick fix, it's an investment in your ministry and your community. There's a learning curve, no doubt. But when you're eyeballing 20-50 fresh faces in your church month after month, all that time and money you poured in is totally worth it, hands down.

And hey, the Shotgun Method doesn't just save you a dime – it's a money-saver in the grand scheme of things. Why? 'Cause you're picking up the knack for what ads strike gold in your neck of the woods. That means each new ad becomes a sniper shot, more tar-geted and even more triumphant than the last. With time, you'll dial back on ad expenses, 'cause each ad will reel in more folks.

In the same breath, the Shotgun Method isn't con-fined to one platform. Don't put all your eggs in a single basket. My two cents? Roll out both Facebook and Instagram ads. These platforms aim at differ-ent crowds, and you've got to test the waters to see where the action's lies in your hood.

Now that you're tuned into the Shotgun Method, it's time to swing back to that all-important question: "What's the right ad budget?" Well, I've got your back. I've whipped up a free resource to help you crack the code. Head over to our website with our nifty calculator at **churchcandy.com/calculator** to lay your hands on the ChurchCandy Ad Spend Budget

Calculator. Plus, there's a free tutorial video to walk you through the ropes.

In order to use the ChurchCandy Ad Spend Budget Calculator, you need to know how many new guests you want each month. Then we'll work backward from there to figure out how much you'll need to spend to get that many visitors to your church.

Here's another number that needs your attention – the average count per family unit in your church. Now, there's a quirky yet effective way to nail this down – simply tally up the people in each car in your parking lot. Yep, it might seem odd, but bear with me. The drill is to divide the total number of attendees at a Sunday service by the number of cars gracing your parking lot.

At Vibrant Church, our magic number per car is 2.4 guests. So, for every person who decides to plan a visit, you're effectively bringing in 2.4 new faces through our doors.

You also need to get a grip on your show rate – the percentage of planned visitors who actually make it. In our case, at Vibrant, our show rate sits comfortably between 70% to 90% thanks to our Plan Your Visit ads. If you're new to the ad game, let's play it safe and estimate a conservative 30% show rate.

Oh, and there's one more number to jot down – the average cost to reel someone in for a visit. This digit's a bit of a chameleon, shifting based on your geographical location and how many local small businesses are dabbling in Facebook ads. Across all the churches I've teamed up with, the ballpark average is around $20 each. Toss that $20 coin into the Facebook ads well, and you'll snag yourself a brand-new family ready to plan a visit.

Quick side note: When you're just starting out, your cost per Plan Your Visit ad might hover on the higher end. But remember – the Shotgun Method will pitch in and chip away at that cost over time. Once you've fine-tuned your ads and mastered what plays best in your neighborhood, you'll be shelling out less for each successful ad.

Let me walk you through an example:

Imagine your goal is to have 50 guests in a month. (We'll round answers to whole numbers for simplicity's sake.)

- You take the number of guests (50) divided by the number of people in each car (2.4).

    - $50 / 2.4 \approx 21$
    - You need approximately 21 people to plan a visit and show up with their families.

- Now you multiply 21 by 3.33 because you have a 30% show rate.

    - 21 x 3.33≈ 70
    - You need 70 families to plan a visit for 21 carloads to show up.

- And since it costs $20 to get each family to plan a visit, you multiply $20 by 70 people for the total cost.

    - $20 x 70 = $1400
    - You'll need to spend $1400 a month to get 50 new guests.

- Facebook ads are paid on a daily basis so if you run it 30 days a month, you'll pay about $46.67 a day.

    - $1,400 / 30= $46.67

- If the Shotgun Method made you 12 ads, you're paying $3.89 per ad, per day.

    - $46.67 / 12= $3.89.

That's about average for us. Most of our ads per day range between $2.00 and $5.00 each.

For many pastors, the thought of welcoming 10 to 20 new guests per month is a cause for celebration. And guess what's even more awesome? The calculator and the Shotgun Method are here to customize those numbers to perfectly fit your church's goals and budget. Plus, if you boost your show rate and lower your cost per PYV, the results could be even more remarkable.

I get it, the calculator might seem a tad puzzling at first, but trust me, it packs a punch when it comes to steering your budget and winning over your elders and leadership team. With this tool in your belt, you'll be equipped to make well-informed decisions about your church's financial allocation.

So, are you ready to untangle the mystery of your ad budget? Head over to churchcandy.com/calculator and let's get the ball rolling!

CHAPTER 13

FOLLOW UP STRATEGIES FOR RETAINING NEW GUESTS

Now that we're successfully drawing people to our services, how do we get them to come back for an encore the following week?

I've got this strong belief that the secret between being just okay and being awesome is speed – how fast you move. So, here we are, embracing a principle that's near and dear to my heart. Over at ChurchCandy, we're all about being the wingman for churches in the business of attracting fresh faces. We're talking about playing the field on platforms like Facebook, Instagram, and Google – that's where we shine. Our aim? To help churches score more visitors for their services.

Pastors often come up to me after a few great services with a worried look and say, "Hey Brady, we had a visitor, but they didn't come back the second week (or third week)." Now, I could think, "Well, I did my part; the rest is up to you," but I understand where they're coming from. If you're really good at getting people to come but find it hard to keep them connected, you're actually doing better than many others. Some churches tell me, "Once people show up, they stay, but getting them to come in the first place is really tough."

So, yes, roping in those guests for the first round is the real test. But let me tell you, keeping them coming back is no piece of cake either. It takes an equal amount of hard work and discipline. Let's roll up our sleeves and dive into it.

Here's a scenario: someone steps foot into your church, and there's this rumor that you've got a teeny window of seven minutes to make a killer first impression before they start judging whether to swing by again next week. Now, I'm on board with this concept, often linked to the wise Carrie Newhoff. But, here's the thing – we might be missing the mark if we go all in on that ticking clock. Sure, having pro greeters in the parking lot and flashy "welcome" signs is all nice and good, but what really matters is weaving that personal connection together to make an impression that lasts.

Sure, those warm grins and breezy "You're part of the gang!" greetings have their place in each church. But let's think about it like this: you walk into Walmart – doors open like magic, and a friendly gray-haired soul gives you a nod. But if you don't build up that sense of community and connection pronto, your guests might just decide to ghost you. While nailing the basics is, well, basic, the real wizardry is in creating actual bonds, making folks feel valued, acknowledged, and like they've got a voice.

Now, let's switch gears and tackle the follow-up game for newbies. If your aim is to make them feel like VIPs rather than a number, what's the play to up your odds of them being repeat customers? That's where a super specific game plan struts onto the scene.

True, plenty of churches are firing off emails or even texts to the rookies, but sometimes it's like a robot talking, and people feel like they're just another number in a system. So, here's my hot tip: dial up the personal touch, show them real warmth and genuine care during their visit. That means stepping up and doing something that sets your ministry in a league of its own.

This isn't about outshining other churches like it's a contest. It's about facing the fact that when folks step into your church, they might be carrying some battle scars from past church experiences. You see, most of the hurt tied to church stuff comes from feeling like you're in invisible mode, like you're talking to a wall. If you tackle this head-on from their very first visit, you're already setting the stage for some top-tier returns and retention.

That's why I made this playbook for making someone feel seen and appreciated, not just being another face in the crowd. Here's the double-feature strategy:

First up is the magic of sending personalized videos, but with a twist – these videos need to be tailor-made for each person. Forget about the cookie-cutter "About Our Church" videos. How about this: every Monday or Tuesday, the pastor records a personal video, dropping names of each family like it's a reunion, and shoots it their way. There are lots of ways to pull this off, like having a designated spot to hit record.

Let's break this down in a way that feels like we're having a casual yet professional chat over coffee. We're in the business of church planting, and you're about to uncover some game-changing techniques. You've got pastors stepping in, and they're getting all these videos done in one go. The trick is to film them in a batch and then hand it over to a team member for exporting. But here's the slick part – send it to the person privately, no public display. A handy tool for this could be loom.com, a website that will undoubtedly make your life easier.

I use this in our businesses all the time. It's a smooth move to make a video. Most folks use it for screen sharing, like recording your screen with a tiny webcam window at the bottom. But, listen up, here's where you could score big – use Loom to record a video directly from your webcam. Plus, if you're aiming for better quality than what your webcam offers, try linking up your iPhone to a Mac and using it as a webcam.

You could also roll with the Loom app on your phone. A lot of the pastors we work with use Church Funnels feature for sending videos through links. But the key here is to keep it simple. If there's a mountain of steps to climb just to send a video, you'll probably never do it.

That's where SOPs (Standard Operating Procedures) come in. If you're dealing with a bunch of families showing up on a Sunday, maybe 20 fresh faces, and you need to send 20 videos, you'll want a solid plan to follow. Now, a video that goes something like, "Hey, John, this is Pastor Brady from Vibrant Church. It was great to see you on Sunday, man!" is simple but it goes a long way towards building lasting and important connections.

You can keep it super casual. Just mention that there's another service next Sunday at either 9:15 or 11 o'clock. Offer to lend a hand and let them know you're praying for them. And just like that, you've got a video that's around 15 seconds – short and sweet. The magic here is making folks feel acknowledged. And here's why it's extra special if it's coming straight from your lead pastor.

Whether you're reeling in one new face or a hundred, when your lead pastor steps up to bat with these videos, it's got a bigger impact. To make it work like a charm, you need a solid SOP. A step-by-step guide to follow, otherwise, it's like a ship without a rudder. So, if you've got a bunch of videos to record, set aside some dedicated time, get Loom ready on your computer, and maybe have an assistant on deck to help with the admin stuff.

You'll be the star of the show, just hit record, stop, and let those warm words flow. Your assistant can handle the rest – transferring those Loom files to texts or wherever they need to land. And speaking of texting, that's a top pick for sending these gems. Email's cool and all, but let's be real, texts have a better shot at being seen.

And now, we need to bring back physical mail to the table – it's like a rare gem these days. Back in the day, we were drowning in mail, but now it's a different story. So, if you have the time, a handwritten thank-you card, done the old-school way, is truly priceless. It doesn't have to be the lead pastor; someone from your team could totally handle this. Write up that card, pop in a $5 gift card to a local coffee shop (if at all possible, try to avoid Starbucks to go with something more unique). Plus, supporting local businesses is a sweet bonus. And here's the kicker – this move can totally make people feel valued, like their visit truly mattered. A little personal touch goes a long way.

Let's break it down – this whole deal is pretty neat because it can come straight from the pastor's corner. You could get them to pen it or just have someone do the honors on behalf of your pastor. The cool part? It gives people that warm feeling of being acknowledged.

The only thing to be wary of is authenticity. People might wonder, "Did Pastor Brady actually write this? Did it really come from him?" And you've got to be on the ball with this. Have those letters prepped and ready, just slot in the family's name and you're good to go. Come Sunday, pop them in the mail. Or you could kick it up a notch – slap a stamp on it, give it that genuine mail look, and drop it in their mailboxes on Monday.

Or here's an idea – have a staffer do the legwork. If you're diving into mail mode, speed is your wingman. Don't let it drag till Wednesday; by then, it's all water under the bridge. They've probably made their mind up about Sunday plans. Again, speed is the name of the game.

So, those are the two aces up your sleeve for boosting retention. And yeah, it goes without saying, have your A-game on when they step through that door. A service that's memorable – incredible worship, a message that's not just fluff, and a staff who is sensitive to the Holy Spirit – that's where the magic happens. It's impactful, it's life-changing.

These two tricks are the gems that most churches overlook. Implementing these could work wonders, bridging the gap between these people and an encounter with Jesus.

CHAPTER 14

BUILDING A CONCIERGE TEAM

At ChurchCandy, we help churches get new guests with Facebook and Instagram ads. The nuts and bolts of that process involve what's called lead generation for churches. We run ads to find people in their community who are interested in attending their church. When someone sees the ad and plans a visit to the church's Sunday service, that person becomes a lead for the church. A lead is a sales term, but we're using it here because we believe in applying the wisdom used in business to grow the kingdom. When someone sees an ad on Facebook, fills out a form, and plans a visit, it's a win, but it doesn't guarantee they'll show up on Sunday.

The key factor here is intent. If someone goes to Google, searches for your church, and plans a visit through your website, their intent is clear—they were actively looking for a church. Therefore, the show rate for people who plan a visit via Google is higher.

In contrast, people on Facebook and Instagram are not necessarily looking for a church, but our ads are designed to attract them. The volume of leads from Facebook and Instagram is high, but the show rate can be low, often around 10-20%.

That was Pastor Ken's experience when he first started with ChurchCandy. Pastor Ken leads a church in Plano, Texas. At the time, they had about 150 people attending. He saw the same 10-20% show rate, which translated to 3-4 new families showing up each week—a significant win for most churches of that size. However, Pastor Ken recognized the potential. If 10-20% were showing up, what about the other 80-90%? These people didn't accidentally click on the ads, plan a visit, and fill out their information. There was a reason they did that. Pastor Ken knew there was a disconnect between the time someone planned a visit online and actually showing up on Sunday.

In this chapter, we'll discuss how they bridged that gap and dramatically increased their show rates, growing their church from 150 people to over 600 in just six months. Their strategy revolves around creating a personal connection with every single person who plans to visit, and doing so quickly. As soon as a form submission comes through, someone from the concierge team reaches out.

When someone fills out that form to plan a visit, they are most interested right then. A study from Harvard shows how the speed of follow-up determines lead conversion rates. Although this is a sales and business stat, we can apply the same metrics to churches. Speed of follow-up is crucial. Pastor Ken built a volunteer team called the concierge team. This team is responsible for following up with every person who plans a visit to their church.

The first step is ensuring follow-up happens quickly. If someone plans a visit in the middle of the night, touch base with them the next morning. But during normal hours, if someone plans a visit, it's imperative they receive a phone call within the first two to five minutes. Using volunteers' personal cell phones instead of a software like ChurchModels increases the answer rate. If they don't answer, volunteers can leave a voicemail and send a follow-up text message. Personal touches like these—blue bubbles on iPhones—can make a significant difference.

Here's the process:

1. Someone plans a visit.
2. Give them a call. If they don't answer, call again immediately. If they still don't answer, leave a voicemail.

3. Send them a text message if they didn't answer after the voicemail.
4. Continue a conversation and build a genuine connection

The goal is to make the interaction feel personal and welcoming, not automated or mundane. In the world of megachurches, one of the biggest reasons people leave is because they feel like just a number, without personal connections to anyone on staff or leadership. This strategy creates an opportunity for people to feel welcomed before they ever step foot on your church's campus.

"Seven minutes is all you get to make a positive first impression. In the first seven minutes of contact with your church, your first-time guests will know whether or not they are coming back. That's before a single worship song is sung and before a single word of the message is uttered." **Fusion** by Nelson Searcy (2007), p49

Nelson Searcy wrote that your church has seven minutes to make a good first impression once someone pulls onto your campus before they make a decision on whether or not they're coming back next week. This strategy takes that a step further, creating a great first experience before people even show up to church.

Here's a script the concierge team uses for following up with people who plan to visit. For big events like Easter and Christmas, they create a large database of everyone who ever planned a visit but didn't show up, and the concierge team reaches out to invite them to the upcoming events. Personal follow-up beats automated follow-up every time. Green bubble text messages and emails can only go so far; personal touches make people feel valued.

<u>Step One:</u> Contact the guest using the number provided.

<u>Step Two:</u> (If Guest Answers): Proceed with the welcome script.

<u>Step Three</u>: If no answer after two calls, send the below text

<u>If Guest Doesn't Answer:</u>

"Hi, my name is [Your Name]. I'm with the concierge team of Connect Church Plano. We noticed you scheduled a visit with us for Easter Sunday. In an effort to ensure your experience is seamless, we have just a few questions for your registration. Feel free to call or text me at this number. Have a blessed day."

<u>Step Five:</u> Click the link provided and complete the registration form. Ensure you click "submit" before dismissing the call.

<u>Step Six:</u> Inform the guest that they will receive an email confirmation.

<u>Step Seven:</u> Thank them for their time and express excitement about meeting them and their family.

<u>Welcome Script:</u>

Hi, my name is [Your Name], and I'm with the concierge team of Connect Church Plano. We are genuinely thrilled that you've chosen to spend Easter with us this weekend. Our goal is to ensure that your experience with us is nothing short of excellent. To start off, we'd like to get all the pertinent details concerning the service you plan to attend and answer any questions you might have.

We're offering three identical ninety minute services throughout the day, each carefully crafted to provide an uplifting and meaningful Easter celebration. So, which service are you planning to attend—8:30 a.m., 10:30 a.m., or 12:30 p.m.?

Additionally, could you please confirm the email we have on file for you? The email we currently have listed is

[State the email you have in the system]. Does that sound correct to you?

FAQ: Why do I have to RSVP?

Response: *"Easter is one of our highest attended services of the year, and we want to be sure we have room for everyone! It's our desire for every attendee to have an amazing experience, and your RSVP helps us to do just that. An RSVP lets us know which service you are planning to attend. All you need to do is select a service time, let us know how many are in your group, and if you have children attending."*

FAQ: Does an RSVP ensure I get a seat?

Response: *"Your RSVP helps us to gauge attendance, not reserve a seat. There are no seat numbers, and nothing to show when you arrive."*

FAQ: What happens if I arrive late, even with an RSVP?

Response: *"Once the Worship Center is at capacity, we will open seats in the overflow area, although it is our desire to seat everyone we can in the main sanctuary."*

FAQ: What is the dress code?

Response: *"Wear whatever you're most comfortable in! Connect Church is a casual church, but on Easter weekend, it's not uncommon to see people dressed up, ready to smile for a photo at one of our photo spots."*

FAQ: What will my kids do while I am in the worship service?

Response: *"Connect Church Kids offers engaging, dynamic programming for babies – 5th grade. They experience a unique worship service, designed just for them, with worship, teaching, and small group time. Easter weekend will feature special interactive activities that your children are guaranteed to LOVE!"*

One of the hardest parts of building this concierge team is recruiting volunteers. It starts with teaching the why. If you can get your volunteers bought into the mission and cast a compelling vision, it's much easier to get them on board. Emphasize the next steps people will take, the marriages that will be saved, the souls that will be won for the Kingdom, the potential baptisms that will come from this effort, etc.

We encourage every church that signs up for Church-Candy to build their own concierge team. Personal follow-up is key to getting those people who plan to visit to actually show up on Sunday. If you want to learn more, Pastor Ken and I recorded a podcast where he shared his story and broke everything down. Be sure to check that out using this QR Code.

FINAL THOUGHTS

I love church plants. They're honestly my favorite clients to work with. If God has called you to plant a church, I want to remind you of Romans 8:28.

And we know that all things work together for good to them that love God, to them who are the called according to his purpose.

We often forget the back half of that verse when it's quoted. If you're called to plant a church, God will work it together for good. The road to church planting is not an easy one by any means. But it's important work that makes a hug impact.

At ChurchCandy, we would love to partner with you to help you build your launch team, launch big, and get new guests every Sunday after launch.

You can hear success stories from other church planters and schedule a discovery call with my team at churchcandy.com/plant

We're thankful for ChurchCandy helping us through our launch process, and now my phone keeps buzzing with other people that are planning their visit!

Brian Bullock
Union Church Charlotte
1700+ on Launch Sunday

We were supposed to do a mailer campaign, but there was a disaster on the printing floor and the mailer didn't go out. Thankfully with the work we did with ChurchCandy, we still had 457 people show up to launch Sunday

Austin Scott
The Heritage Co Church
457 on Launch Sunday

ChurchCandy has been instrumental to the growth of our church! More than 80% of our church came through the ads that ChurchCandy set up for us!

Jason Shepherd
Illuminate Church
125+ on Launch Sunday

ChurchCandy was game changer for our launch! We partnered with them right before our grand opening Sunday, and they helped us get over 400 people to show up!

Paul Miller
HopeX Church
400+ on Launch Sunday

We have seen so many great people respond; that don't know the Lord, that have questions about their faith. We're thankful for ChurchCandy to help us get connected with all of these people!

Clayton Smalls
The Ark Magnolia
750+ on Launch Sunday

99% of our church heard about us from Facebook and Instagram ads because of ChurchCandy!

Joe Angelo
Vivid Church
225 on Launch Sunday

ChurchCandy has been incredible to work with! They helped us grow our launch team, launch big, and get tons of guests post launch with their ads!

Derrick Hawkins
Promise City Church
950 on Launch Sunday

Planting a church in Montana is not easy! ChurchCandy was able to get us connected with hundreds of families we wouldn't have known otherwise!

Todd Nicholson
Buffalo Church
150+ on Launch Sunday

187

ChurchCandy saved our church plant! Our first two interest parties flopped because we couldn't get people to show up when we did our own ads.

Brandon Holmes
Promise Co Church
200+ on Launch Sunday

Launch Sunday was fantastic! There were so many people there because of ChurchCandy!

Steve Quint
Monroe City Church
350+ on Launch Sunday

We're so thankful we partnered with ChurchCandy! We had over 450 people show up on Launch Sunday

Alfredo Rosado
The Father's House Elk Grove
480 on Launch Sunday

We would love to help your church or church plant grow with social media. View more success stories & schedule a free discovery call at churchcandy.com/plant

Printed in the USA
CPSIA information can be obtained
at www.ICGtesting.com
LVHW010151061024
792988LV00015B/1114